# EDUCATION THROUGH TRAVEL

Barbara
A.
Ainsworth

**Nelson-Hall** nh **Chicago**

Library of Congress Cataloging in Publication Data

Ainsworth, Barbara A.
  Education through travel.

  Bibliography:   p.
  Includes index.
  1.  Travel.  I.  Title.
ISBN 0-88229-365-6 (cloth)
ISBN 0-88229-693-0 (paper)

Manufactured in the United States of America.

10      9      8      7      6      5      4      3      2      1

In loving memory of
Pete

# Contents

# Preface

This book resulted from two challenging experiences. As a teacher, I wanted to show the world to my students. As a mother, I wanted to teach the world to my children. So much to see, so much to learn—and the joy of exploring the world as a family, or with a group of students, made each trip a creative experience.

Often, friends would question our frequent family jaunts. The children traveled with us as infants, as toddlers, and as growing curious children. The idea of leaving them behind and missing the joy of family discovery was unthinkable. We traveled by car, bus, plane, and train. We camped in farmers' yards, in deluxe campsites, in motels, and in the Conrad Hilton Hotel. We went for fun, for business, and for family visiting. At one point, we converted a large school bus into a camper and we became a family educational team on wheels. Each of us pursued personal interests but shared in the total group understanding and pleasure.

I gratefully acknowledge the aid and advice of my four companions in travel: Pete, a patient husband and father; and our children, David, John, and Mary Virginia. I also am grateful for the help of Dr. Floyd A. Pace, Buena Vista College. He listened to my ideas, encouraged my enthusiasms, and corrected my manuscript. For technical assistance, interesting ideas, and shared concerns, I extend thanks to Carol Wagner.

# Why Not Take the Kids?

A gray house rests on a high bank of the Mississippi under large shade trees, cool and inviting on a hot summer day. Attractive girls in long dresses meet you at the door and carefully explain the 1901 vintage furnishings. The home (Figure 1.1) belonged to C. A. Lindbergh, Minnesota lawyer, U.S. Congressman, and father of Lucky Lindy.

The home is carefully preserved. Visitors can see the shell collections of the younger Lindbergh, his saddle, his toy soldiers, and the car he drove to California before the age of interstate speed and convenience. His mother's china, collected from all over the world, sits on the dining room table, and in the kitchen squats the woodburning stove.

It takes two hours to tour this house, the Lindbergh Interpretive Center, and to hear about three generations of the remarkable Lindberghs.

Figure 1.1.   Boyhood home of Charles Lindbergh

The children move between the cases at the Center, under the trees, across the swinging bridge (a replica of an earlier Lindbergh construction), and up the stairs of the family home.

Later someone asks, "What did you see?" The eleven-year-old remembers the pictures of an "airplane or something," the seven-year-old "liked the old car," and the five-year-old "had fun with the little chipmunk because the girl in the long dress let me feed it some peanuts."

But who was Lindbergh?

"A man."

"He flew across some water—a big lake, I think."

"A little boy who played with old toys."

Dumb kids? Not really—just typical children of tourists. Is it really important that a five-year-old know about Lindbergh? Maybe not. How about a seven-year-old or an eleven-year-old? If it doesn't matter for children to know the "who" or "when" of what they see, then why bother to traipse them through the exhibits?

This question points directly to the problem of vacation planning in many American homes. Dad wants to play golf and Mom wants to sightsee a little and shop for souvenirs. The kids want to go to Disneyland because they saw it on TV. Once Dad scratches Disneyland on the basis of finances and distance, the kids probably have little knowledge about what's available in the area they will visit. Is it possible to please the whole family? Maybe the kids should go to camp while Mom and Dad travel. After all, what can a kid get out of a trip anyway?

A great deal.

Every experience available to a child is loaded with potential learning possibilities. A family trip is a vehicle for exploration of new places, new people, and new ideas. How far and in what direction the exploration goes is often dependent on the adult who is there at the time.

But even alone, a child in a new situation learns.

Remember the children in the Lindbergh house? Did they learn anything? Suppose they were asked some different questions. For example: "What's the difference between this house and the one you live in?" and "Why did the people who lived here choose this place?" and "Suppose Mr. Lindbergh were sitting in that chair again—what would you ask him?"

Whether or not such questions are asked, whether or not the experience is planned and guided, a child's world is broadened when he steps

3

on new turf, views new places, and bumps into new people. Quite simply, a child classifies knowledge as things *like* home and those *unlike* home. Beyond that, children evaluate new things they encounter. "Ah, this place is *better* than home," or, "Ugh! This food is much *worse* than what Mom cooks." Contrasting and comparing are two skills which are sharpened by new experiences.

Family relationships are reinforced during shared vacation trips—for better or for worse. If you have difficulty playing the role of the kind, understanding, patient parent at home, a change of scene will probably have little effect on your image. If discipline is lacking on the home front, reform will probably not occur on a trip. You are what you are and your children know it. Whatever makes your family work at home will continue to make it work on the road. One learning opportunity for your children lies in extra vacation time to view family relationships in action. The working members of the household aren't missing from nine to five o'clock.

In addition, new situations uncover new aspects of the same old family members. To the youngest children, Mom and/or Dad represent home security in new settings, making it safe to explore new environments. Older children see decision-making processes operating in their family. Who decides what route to take, where and when to eat, whether to stop at the amusement park? And how is the inevitable vacation crisis handled? How does Daddy react when his wallet is stolen or the tire goes flat? What does Mom do? In a strange place, are the rules or procedures different from those which operate at home? Probably not, and so older children gain some security from the sameness of their family in a strange new place.

Family values are learned by children on a trip. What makes Dad and Mom happy—the cocktail lounge or the pool? What are top priority activities during leisure time away from the home? What's the purpose of the trip?

Children *do* learn valuable things on a trip. "Should we take the kids?" is a personal and important question. How much do you want your child to know about the things you plan to do on your trip? Do you want your child to learn more about you and the things you like to do? Then, by all means, why not take the kids!

But, before we go any further let's take a . . .

## TRAVELOGUE VIEW OF THE BOOK

Most people travel through a book in a logical fashion; that is, as the Queen of Hearts explained to Alice, they begin at the beginning and stop when they reach the end.

Yet there are plenty of people who thumb through magazines backwards. Some years ago, a ladies' magazine featured the table of contents in the back to accommodate these folk. Although it was an imaginative idea, its lack of success proves that, though some people approach printed matter in different ways, they still expect to find things in traditional places. Nevertheless, no two people will approach this book with the same needs and interests. This guided tour will help you plan your reading according to your particular requirements.

Are you a parent planning the annual two-week family jaunt? You could easily skip the theoretical section and move directly to the practical suggestions in Chapters 6 through 14. Are you worried about the educational potential of your child? Is school difficult for him or her? Or, maybe school is too easy for your talented youngster, and he needs new experiences to keep up his interest. Again, you'll want to look through some of the ideas in Chapters 6 through 14. Perhaps you're willing to spend some extra preparation time in order to provide a more intensive experience for your child. You've decided he or she needs more attention and you're the only one to provide it. A number of the ideas in these chapters are somewhat complicated and require additional time and materials. You may find an idea or two that will help you in your goals. Perhaps you are a teacher facing the annual field trip challenge. The students are pushing for the greatest distance and the most fun. Somehow you're determined to make it an educational experience. Chapter 5 will provide the academic framework for your planning. Then look in Chapters 3 and 4 for the theoretical framework underlying the practical ideas to follow.

Are you a single parent, wondering if a trip is worth the trouble? Can you handle it alone? Being a single parent means that you and the kids have your own thing going. You have opportunities for joint planning and for close relationships built through memory gathering. As a single parent you may have more flexibility. Or, the travel experience may be part of brief visitation time with your children and you're anxious to make the most of it. One of the greatest blocks to "making the most of it" is the anxiety you feel in meeting the desires of your children. It's overcompensation time; but as soon as you get into that game, you are all bound to lose. The secret is to analyze your children's interests, and focus attention on these interests during advance planning and during the progress of the trip. You may wish to read about childhood developmental phases in Chapter 3 and preplanning ideas in Chapter 4 before examining the practical ideas in the remaining chapters.

Are you a concerned school administrator, curriculum coordinator, or parent who seeks educational justification for field trip activities? You'll find some help in Chapters 4 and 5 which should be useful to you.

Pick and choose—search for the useful in every experience—whether it's a trip on the road or a tour through a book.

# 2

# A Trip Is Like a Pot of Stew

In everyday life, all kinds of experiences—tastes, smells, sounds, and sights—combine as a kaleidoscope of stimuli. A trip heightens these sensations; we become more aware of experiences than we are in ordinary life. The difference lies in the fact that ordinary, everyday life experiences are taken for granted. Trip events are new; they sharpen our focus and our awareness.

Daily life depends on knowledge gained from many different sources. A child is a new adventurer in the world, a world which adults often separate into different academic disciplines. Children do not see the world in terms of these separate and narrow distinctions. They live in an interdisciplinary world. A trip provides a mosaic of experiences beyond their familiar ground. Once a child experiences and gains interest in this wider world, he can then be introduced to the content and questions of various academic disciplines for possible further study, if he so chooses.

A trip is like a pot of stew. We can focus on the ingredients: the potatoes, carrots, the bits of meat. Each part is intriguing, but cooked together they form a lovely whole—a tasty pot of stew. A family trip can be viewed in the same way. New experiences, gathered in new places, combine as a "new reality," a whole formed of many different parts.

Learning involves discovering relationships between ingredients, between the parts and the whole, and between separate wholes. The motivation that generally causes a person to search for these relationships is the discovery of a set of facts packaged as a problem.

This discovery process is called *heuristics*, a word derived from a Greek word meaning "to discover." It's a way of thinking one step beyond the exact message delivered by the evidence. Heuristic thought involves making a hypothesis or generalization to account for a collection of facts. For example, a child might tour an autumn forest, learning different habits and characteristics of the species that live there, and emerge with a new understanding of relationships between facts about trees, birds, and the seasons. Heuristic learning is natural on a trip.

Many commonplace problems are routinely solved on a trip. Where do we sleep? What time should we stop for a meal? Should we see the museum this afternoon or linger beside the pool? More intellectual problems can be discussed as well. How much faster are we able to cross the plains than the early settlers? Why were the Indians sometimes hostile and sometimes friendly?

9

These routine and intellectual problems are easily answered in an acceptable, expected manner. Two plus two equals four, right? But what about the person who comes up with an unexpected answer. Is that person wrong? Or does the "strange" solution suggest a touch of creativity?

Some experts have argued that creativity cannot be taught; either it exists in an individual or it doesn't. Others disagree. Certainly, exposure to a variety of objects and ideas is bound to expand thinking abilities.

What's the difference between a creative solution and a nutty idea? The true measure of a creative idea lies in its originality, its development and, of course, its success. Will it work, in spite of the fact that it's unusual? Of course, creative ideas aren't always socially acceptable, either! Nevertheless, if your child comes up with an uncommon idea, don't cut him off at the pass with a negative reaction. Help him explore the idea, remembering the trial-and-error process in learning. The pot of stew that your child stirs up may have a different flavor, but that doesn't mean it isn't tasty.

We need some specific examples of heuristic thinking and creative responses. While no trip is exactly like any other, similar ideas may be developed in different circumstances. Some themes which could be used to unify observations and ideas include: pollution, ecology, transportation, energy, landforms, architecture, and differences in people. Each of these topics can be discussed in terms of a specific discipline, but basically they are interdisciplinary and can refer to a number of trip experiences.

Surely it's a rare family that sets out on a vacation together for the avowed purpose of examining the causes and effects of pollution! Of course, it is possible, and such a plan can unite like-minded family members into a cohesive group of researchers. Nevertheless, most thematic trips simply develop from a combination of factors, like those things seen from the car window and the discussion of them that follows.

A child's curiosity raises questions which many adults choose to ignore or answer too quickly. Instead, they might guide the child to look more carefully for clues and ideas which form a pattern. The developing creativity of a child may restructure an apparently obvious pattern. Instead of passing a negative judgment or resorting to the quick answer, ask the child further questions which would test the validity of his new pattern of ideas.

"Where is the train going, Daddy?" A child's question or a childish question? Daddy's opinion on that will color his reply. If he accepts it as an opportunity to aid his child's intellectual exploration, he might say, "Well, I'm not sure. What clues do we have?" A joint consideration of available facts might follow while they review: (1) the compass direction of the train's movement; (2) the type of railroad cars; (3) the writing on the sides of some railroad cars; and (4) the possible destinations on the map which appear to lie in the same compass direction. Maybe they will never know the true answer to where that train is going, but the child has learned, among other things, two valuable things: (1) Dad values his ideas; and (2) even know-it-all Dad looks to other sources of information before making a good guess.

Extending a brief question into an entire interdisciplinary study can be a bit tedious for all concerned. But a series of questions about trains and trucks and airplanes can develop into a comparison of transportation modes and their relative consumption of time and energy. It can be a very casual thing, but some older children will want to find specific answers in an encyclopedia when they get home. Such interest should be encouraged by having them write out their questions for later referral.

Most interdisciplinary questions don't have to be forced—they just appear, and can be developed only if we recognize them.

It is morning and we are in a new motel. *Geographically*, we can find its location on a map. The motel is across the street from the café where we will probably have breakfast, located in a town which is supported by some kind of industry and populated by people who do some kind of work in relation to the land on which the town is located. *Historically*, someone, somewhere, sometime decided to build this town, this motel, and that café across the street. People have lived here, made money, lost money, laughed, loved, and died. *Sociologically*, the townspeople live together in patterns of human behavior which are familiar anyplace, and yet, with tiny idiosyncracies that are peculiar to this particular place. *Politically*, they govern themselves in a particular way, and *ecologically* they attempt to reach a balance between their human activities and the natural habitat.

The child waking in the bed in the motel room certainly does not separate these facts into neat little disciplinary boxes. Nor do his parents consciously think in terms of these categories. What they do naturally is *synthesize* experiences, facts, and knowledge into a "stew" made of parts of many disciplines.

The light patterns on the ceiling which greet Mary as she wakes in the motel room give her clues to the kind of day outside. A new place has new smells and feelings, and since Mom and Dad are here, none of these smells or tastes are labeled "bad" in her five-year-old mind. At breakfast in the local café, Johnny looks around and says, "This place is funny!" What does he mean? Is it because there are many different kinds of pancake syrup on the table? Is it that all the tables are round and placed in the center of the room and there aren't any booths as in restaurants at home? Is it because the waitress seems half-asleep and when he ordered hot chocolate, she brought him white milk instead? Is it the strange sights he can see beyond the plate glass window with "Café" written backwards in neon?

The truth is that this new place *is* a different place—"a funny place." Its strangeness could be defined in terms of mathematical dimensions, historical perspectives, sociological influences, or even psychological attitude perceptions. But the narrow pursuit of each discipline would eliminate the contributions of the others.

It's difficult to relate interdisciplinary experiences to knowledge acquired through the study of separate disciplines. We rarely express ourselves in those formal terms. But, in order to begin to learn about this new place and the reasons why it appears "funny" to a child, we must be more specific, more descriptive.

"Johnny, tell me all the things here that appear 'funny' to you," is a request that may result in a brief or lengthy list of oddities which contrast with the familiarities of home. Johnny's original statement may be a fleeting reaction or it may be a symptom of basic confusions. It's necessary for his parents to follow his trail of thought and to encourage him to set out on his own trail of investigation.

Before we launch into specific activity suggestions, a few preliminary preparations could be made. A small box of materials for the back seat crew will be useful in their data-gathering activities. This list of items is only a suggestion; the final decision is determined by your children's capabilities and interests. Consider it a:

## SHOPPING LIST FOR A FAMILY TRIP

- crayons
- \* pencils and small sharpener
- \* scissors
- paste
- scrapbook
- small notebooks—plain and lined paper
- a roll of shelf paper
- \* collection containers: egg cartons, baby food jars, cigar boxes
- \* magnifying glass
- maps
- travel brochures
- paperback nature guides

---

*These items are potentially dangerous in a moving vehicle and their use should be limited to stationary situations.

The most essential items that you'll need to pack are patience and enthusiasm. The former is important in dealing with a child's energies; the latter is the fuel injection periodically required to maintain interest. It's almost guaranteed when you back out of the driveway you'll have left something behind, but hopefully not patience and enthusiasm. With these qualities in tow, the trip will be a success!

# 3

# What Do the Experts Say?

Okay, the family decision is made—the kids get to come along on the next trip. This can be a valuable experience if the family so wishes. Is there any way to be more sure about the decision? Yes, and we can start by consulting the experts. A lot of people have spent much time studying different types of activities and situations which can create or enhance a learning environment.

Learning processes rely on stimulus and response. Children learn by being stimulated; they act in response to stimuli. But some experts question whether this is decision making or merely reaction. Thought processes, they argue, require a framework for decision making—a framework of analysis, if you will. Experiences reflected against the background of previous experience and contrasted with the shared experiences of others provide a wider context for decision making. The ability to make decisions well is an educational goal which most parents seek for their children.

In this chapter, we'll briefly consider the theories and philosophies of three men: Jean Piaget, John Dewey, and Ivan Illich. Separated in time and space, each has contributed something relevant to the topic of education and travel.

Jean Piaget tells us that children learn through experience. Their knowledge, or "structure," is built in developmental stages. A concept gained or understood by a child is a structure which is then used to organize the next piece of information presented to the child. Moreover, as new knowledge is assimilated, it may change the original structure in the child's mind.

Of what relevance are these theories to what happens to a child on a trip? One interpreter of Piaget, John L. Phillips, has attempted to relate theory to classroom teaching. He defines teaching as "the manipulation of the student's environment in such a way that his activities will contribute to his development."[1] A trip is á method by which a parent can manipulate his or her child's environment. Certainly some of the trip activities will contribute to the child's development.

To Piaget, the term "development" actually means a change in the child's intellectual structure or knowledge. Knowledge doesn't come packaged in neat pieces; one is not built right atop another to form an airtight structure. Rather, the arrival of a new idea or experience may conflict with knowledge previously acquired. For example, a toddler is sure that the world moves past the

---

1. John L. Phillips, Jr., *The Origins of Intellect: Piaget's Theory* (San Francisco: Freeman, 1975), p. 140.

stationary window of his car until, as he matures, he discovers conflicting evidence. In order to accommodate the conflict, the structure itself changes. The child "changes his mind." This new whole is more than a simple sum of its parts. Knowledge is not a cumulative "total" of ideas, but results from *constructing* a whole built of experiences and ideas, and assimilating new knowledge with previous experience and ideas.

Several periods of development have been identified by Piaget. Although each is assigned to a specific age group, we know that children develop at different rates. The interesting point, however, is that all children move through these periods in the same order, even if not at the same age.

Piaget calls the first two years of life the "sensorimotor" period. A baby's senses bring him messages about his world—he moves in response to the stimuli around him. At the beginning of this period, the baby recognizes the existence of an object only when it is right before him. Out of sight, out of mind, so to speak. Slowly, he develops the idea that this object continues to exist, even when it is not in his view.

Who could predict the effect of a trip during these first two years, when a child is still discovering and experimenting with sensory messages? Does a baby benefit from a family trip? Let's consider the alternatives. A baby on a family trip sees changing scenery, but his favorite toy, his bottle, and his family members remain constant. A baby left behind with someone else sees familiar scenery but has a new person to care for his needs. An infant who can conceive of objects even when they are out of his sight has a limited ability to recall.

The decision about taking a baby along—if based solely on the trip value for that baby—might be easier for Mom and Dad if the alternatives are examined in light of their possible implications. Which should remain intact for the child—scenery or family?

Piaget labels the next period "preoperational." Older children, between two and seven years, are able to think in terms of symbols, whereas infants only know concrete objects. Words are symbolic of concrete objects. The verbal child can conceive of a past and a future. But in this preoperational period, the child cannot interpret an operation which reverses ideas, or changes shapes but not quantity. One of Piaget's more famous experiments involves pouring an amount of liquid from a short, squat container into a tall cylinder. Preoperational children believe the taller container is holding more water, equating greater height with greater volume. Moreover, the world of a preoperational child must follow *his* rules, or else it's wrong. Any other point of view is initially inconceivable to him.

This period, like all the others, is natural and necessary. No parent or teacher can explain reality in adult terms to a child who has not yet completed the necessary developmental steps. So, why bother? In time, the child will correct his errors. True enough, but providing a preoperational child with a variety of experiences will help him to learn that other ideas and other points of view exist. Things may be shown to be "different" to him, rather than simply "wrong" or "impossible."

The preoperational child may be able to use symbols, but he is still fairly limited to their concrete representations. For example, a child, correctly pronouncing all the syllables in the word "Mississippi," still receives only one picture in his mind as he says it. Furthermore, to see *and* touch, to talk *and* hear, to smell *and* taste are all very important. Trips to new places can increase the ability to experiment with additional concrete objects in concrete situations. A distant place then becomes a reality rather than an abstraction to a preoperational child.

Children between seven and eleven years are capable of what Piaget calls "concrete operations." These mobile intellectual operations include taking different points of view. The older child can focus on more than one quality or aspect of a situation and can see relationships among the different objects or aspects of a single object. To him, the Mississippi River has cause-effect relationships. "The water flows from here to there because . . ." "The people who live near the river can . . ." Concepts of time and space come to have greater meaning.

One of Piaget's experiments deals specifically with time in relation to movement. Time, movement, and velocity are interlocking concepts that most scientists find impossible to separate; yet, they are frequently taught to children as separate concepts. Time, movement, and velocity are all within the experience framework of a trip. A child, exposed to comparative speeds and distances, can be encouraged to ask questions and understand the figures on a map in relation to the figures on the odometer and speedometer.

Between the ages of eleven and fifteen, the child enters the adult world of "formal operations." In this period, the intellect builds upon sensory data and mental operations, and then takes that additional step into the world of "What if . . .?" New combinations of previously learned elements and going beyond known data are now possible. Literary symbolism, inferences, irony—all have meaning. Explorations in science, math, and social science which extend into hypothetical thought occur at this level.

These stages or periods of development are not laid out as hurdles over which we must push our children in order for them to "progress." Each period, in its given order, is a natural part of intellectual development. According to Piaget, knowledge gained by an individual comes from several sources. Only one of those sources, "social transmission," involves learning by listening. A child accepts and believes and acts on knowledge which has been told to him by another person. That person, an adult or a peer, may or may not know what he's talking about, but to the learner he is an "authority" worth hearing. The child learns what he has been told.

Sounds like school, doesn't it? We know the world is round because we saw its picture in a book; we know the color called red because the teacher said it isn't called green. But not all knowledge can be gained through attentive sit-up-and-listen situations.

Knowledge is also acquired through activity in what Piaget calls "physical" experiences and in "logico-mathematical" relationships. The first type of activity is usually observable: touching, bending, scraping, grouping, piling, and sometimes breaking things. Logico-mathematical ac-

21

tivity may be restricted to the mind and is involved with comparing, contrasting, serializing, and mentally rearranging. Obviously, these kinds of knowledge can't be told to a child or handed out like bits of wrapped candy. The child's own physical and mental activity *creates* the knowledge. And here's where we return to Phillips' definition of teaching as "manipulating" a child's environment so that learning results from active involvement.

John Dewey has been a leading expert in the field of education for decades. Dewey's philosophies were proposed early in the century and have appeared periodically in recent decades under new names. His philosophy is the basis of many "new" educational ideas. Education through activity is a major part of that philosophy. In one of his more famous statements, the "Pedagogic Creed," Dewey said, "Education must be conceived as a continuing reconstruction of experience; . . . the process and the goal of education are one and the same thing."[2] Learning, therefore, is valuable in itself. And learning activities take place constantly—in and out of the classroom.

Activity, as these experts describe it, is more than the going-through-the-motions sort of thing frequently found in school labs. Unless the child is actively investigating by asking questions of his or her own design, such activity is no more than a demonstration. The child may be "doing it" by going through the motions of carefully followed directions, but if the experiment is not going to

2. Robert Ulrich, ed., *Three Thousand Years of Educational Wisdom* (Cambridge, Mass.: Harvard Univ. Press, 1954). p. 635.

satisfy a real curiosity, then the activity isn't really valuable to the child.

Dewey pointed out the value of problem solving as a learning method. No matter how simple or how complex a situation, if it is recognized by the individual as a "problem," it is a potential learning situation. The difference between a prescribed activity handed to a child by an adult and a true learning activity is this degree of problem recognition by the individual himself. There's a world of difference between, "Mom said I had to take off the lid from this bottle of castor oil," and "I wonder how I can get the lid off this cookie jar." The difference lies in the level and importance of the problem recognized by the child. Certainly the motivation behind the two activities is different!

Dewey describes specific steps in solving problems, which simplified are: thinking it through; getting an idea; and trying it out.

Both Dewey and Piaget recognize the importance of error. If a child is going to learn by doing, he's going to make mistakes. The mistakes seem so obvious to an adult that it's a rare adult that can stand by and watch them happen without interfering. Piaget says that some types of knowledge just can't be told to a learner, and Dewey says that problems need to be solved *by* the learner, not *for* the learner. If a child is going to learn, he or she must do it alone, and all kinds of mistakes may occur. And each mistake should be a lesson in itself.

Is it safe to allow children to make mistakes on a trip? Imagine a family in which the children read the map and misdirect the driver; sometimes miles may be driven before a mistake is discov-

ered. Not every parent has the money for gas or the patience for that kind of mistake. How involved are the children in this problem? Are they reading the map because an adult doesn't like the job? Or are they individually concerned with solving the problem of reaching a destination by the shortest route? Dewey cautions that problems must grow naturally out of an experience, lie within the capacity of the learner to solve, and raise the learner's interest in an active search for the answer.

A child appears to think randomly and to make decisions sometimes by not making a decision. He goes off in several directions because of momentary interests, and decisions may be based on feelings of the moment and a need for immediate reward. Nevertheless, experiences can be structured so that questions arise naturally, answers are tested, errors are discovered, and alternatives are considered. The answer is less important than the process by which answers are sought.

Dewey thought these structured learning activities were possible within the school system. He stressed a nontraditional approach. Piaget supported this theme and called for improvements in the level of teacher preparation, so that trained adults would be able to structure adaptable environments for the differing intellectual capabilities of children. Ivan Illich and Everett Reimer, two of the more radical experts of our time, suggest on the other hand that we just forget about schools. Illich speaks of webs and Reimer of networks, but both authors are concerned with direct links between the learner and the learning experience. Their plans call for contact with materials (either

directly or through media), a model or skilled worker, and matched peer partners in learning. The role of teacher is changed from a dispenser of knowledge to a guide or contact person through whom learning arrangements are made—that is, if a "teacher" is necessary at all.

Illich and Reimer have social and political reasons for their suggestions. But ignoring their purposes and focusing on their proposed model, one can grasp the central theme of *reality* as the greatest learning environment. Seeing the real thing happening in the real place is better than reading about it in a book. These authors believe in this experience so deeply that they are ready to call for the abolishment of schools. It kind of makes you wonder why most of us are so careful to arrange vacation times which do not conflict with the children's school schedule. "We'd like to tour Canada, but the children are in school then, so we just can't take them." Sounds familiar, doesn't it?

Surely, there's a happy middle ground. But it takes advance planning and a joint, cooperative effort by parents and teachers. Suppose a February business trip provides an opportunity for the family to tour Texas. What can Johnny do about his school work? A creative teacher will prepare well in advance for these types of requests from parents. There's nothing like learning about a trip at three o'clock on Friday afternoon and trying to come up with a week's worth of assignments so that Johnny can keep pace with his class, in spite of his absence! It doesn't work unless some ideas are prepared in advance of the situation. For example, the issue of "covering the text" will have to be resolved beforehand. Also, if a first-hand experience can "teach," then the content of the trip should be considered relevant educational material. The theories and philosophies of the experts we've discussed suggest that it should be possible to discover methods of making a trip an educational experience instead of an interlude followed by meaningless make-up work.

Dewey suggested experience itself can teach, so the assignment issued by the teacher should be flexible enough to capitalize on as yet unknown, distant experiences. Piaget argues only limited forms of knowledge can be transmitted orally, so assignments should be designed to raise questions of comparison which are important to the child and which might launch further investigations. And Illich thinks that all this can happen beyond the walls of the school, beyond the reach of a teacher's voice, and still be meaningful.

It is a wise teacher or parent who provides a framework for upcoming experience, in which events will form a meaningful, interesting pattern. As a child experiences something new, his world expands. Faced with sensory information and armed with rational thinking skills, children make better decisions. Exposure to a wider world multiplies sensory information, and a structural framework provides the means through which rational thinking skills develop.

# 4

# Let's Take a Field Trip

There are many similarities between a school field trip and a family excursion. In both cases, the child is being taken from a familiar environment into a new one. Teachers state that the purpose of leaving the schoolroom walls is to aid children's learning by exposing them to the real world. If parents expressly state their purpose, it is usually to get away, relax, and have a good time together. But the same thing is happening in both situations: the child enters a new world. As we have already noted, the child learns from this new world, regardless of aid or lack of it from adult companions. But if even a casual framework is erected around the experience, the child is bound to learn even more.

Whether planned by Mom and Dad or by Mrs. Jackson, the second-grade teacher, a field trip has certain special elements. First of all, interest is developed in some space, some object, some place beyond the usual daily environment. A new experience is planned by an adult and a child gains a wider view of the world.

A teacher who plans a field trip spends a lot of time making arrangements for learning experiences. She or he hopes that the kids will apply what they've learned in class to this new thing or place they will see. And it's also hoped that contact with a new experience will provide some motivation for kids so they'll want to learn even more.

But why shouldn't the same be true of a family trip? Most family trips include the children because "they'll have fun," but can't learning be fun as well?

Besides exploring a. new area, family and school trips share the element of adult supervision, adult concern, and adult planning. Which brings us to another important element: the sharing of an experience by two different age groups—kids and grownups. Different perspectives on the same experience can be enriching for *all* age groups. How involved both kids and adults become in planning and evaluating the experience is a measure of the value of that experience for each age group.

The assumption here is that the trip destination is "new," but that's not always the case. Trips to Grandma's house are made repeatedly—usually the same route, same time of year, same hour of departure. And what teacher, having announced a field trip, hasn't been faced with, "What? We're going to the museum *again*?" No value in these trips? Oh yes, there is! The key to successful learning on such trips is a new focus, a new view of the familiar, or a new search for the unfamiliar.

Another common element of class trips and family trips is the necessity of a vehicle or some other means of travel which gets the kids to a place they've never been before. The vehicle which takes them there is the medium through which their world is expanded. It's a creative teacher or parent who utilizes the medium to its full educational advantage. Often this element is taken for granted and transportation time is "passed" by concentrating on other things. Songs like "Ninety-Nine Bottles of Beer on the Wall" are indicative of the level of monotony.

Occasionally the vehicle is new to the child and so the transporting experience is heightened without any extra adult planning. A child who lives within walking distance of the school finally gets to ride the big yellow school bus. Or the family decides to trade cost for speed and flies to their destination and the child delights in the feel of flying.

Another common element in trips lies in the framework of time and distance. Quite simply, there is a beginning and an end. Time measured by distance and distance measured by time is unique to traveling. "We'll get from here to there in an hour," and "If it's 10:00 a.m., this must be Toronto," are both unique, trip-type statements. Both measures are new or unfamiliar to a child used to regular, fixed home and school schedules.

These basic elements are found in any trip shared by an adult with a child, so what makes a family trip more valuable? Any adult who has traveled with a school-sponsored field trip recognizes that group camaraderie is merely a trade-off for the separate choices of individuals planning their own trip. It's a jolly, singing bus load that sets off for a distant goal and an exhausted, frequently irritable group that returns. Too much to see, too little time, and too many students with too many individual goals which may or may not be considered educational in terms of the school curriculum.

But a family group is, first of all, smaller and certainly easier to handle. Or is it? How can a rational adult plan on keeping several children of various ages happily occupied? That, of course, is the other main difference between school and family groups—the ages of the children usually vary in the latter. But what appears on first glance as a disadvantage might well enhance an interesting variety of experiences for the entire family.

David has had eleven years of experience in examining his world. How can he find common interests with his quiet, seven-year-old brother, John? After all, Johnny is only a second-grader and he doesn't even remember some of the family memories that David shares with his parents. And then there's Mary. At age five, what can she possibly do on a trip besides complain and whine? Certainly she won't enjoy doing and seeing the same things as John and David!

What makes it possible for such a hodgepodge of ages to get along on a trip? The same things that work at home—a sharing and caring that is rooted at a deeper level than that found among peer group members of different backgrounds. And because the family group is smaller, there is greater flexibility in meeting the individual needs of the separate family members. Certainly over the years, a parent learns far more about his child's needs and interests than a teacher with a one-year commitment to twenty or thirty children.

A family group that listens to its individual members gains as a group and as individuals. For example, Mary found a rock and claimed it as her very own. She liked its shape and smooth surface. John pointed out that it would be a super skipping rock for the lake, if only Mary would let it go. David was interested in its color and wondered if it might be chert, or then again, it might be . . . of course, if only he could get it out of Mary's clutches, he could check it with his rock manual. Potential argument? Right! But also an interesting three-way perspective focused on one object with each child viewing the contested object from a separate vantage point. A five-year-old can learn much while she looks over her brother's shoulder into his rock manual and he tells her a name for "her" rock. And then there's the fun of looking for others of the same shape for skipping. John has a skill that Mary tries hard to acquire. But, can these older, more skillful children learn from a five-year-old? Well, it's been a long while since they appreciated the texture, color, and weight of a rock. Because of Mary's discovery, the boys can appreciate those qualities again. The point is that each child has something to share with the others. If they listen to each other, each can partake of a wider view than the more limited perspective held individually.

Knowledge and skills are only two areas which differ with age. Attitudes can also be shared, and this is the area of greatest contribution by the younger members of the group. The enthusiasm of a discoverer or a first-timer can then be recaptured by the old pros. That which is old, familiar, and taken for granted appears fresh and new seen through the eyes of the youngest one. Older children can teach younger ones the patience and calm attitude of passive observation. Sitting behind a shield of branches to quietly watch wildfowl feed in a lake might take more patience than Mary has learned in her five years. But David's example makes it possible, and both are able to share new experiences (Figure 4.1).

Cross-age grouping is a new idea in education. The concept of sharing abilities and interests across age "barriers" has proven valuable in raising achievement levels for both younger and older students. Motivation also appears improved, particularly among older underachieving students who view their work with younger children as a special responsibility.

But what's so new about cross-age grouping?

Figure 4.1. David and Mary watch wildfowl feed

It's a natural part of family life and it was the typical classroom pattern in the old one-room schoolhouse. Today, when a community is faced with the education of 180 elementary students, it's just more convenient to build six rooms and split the mob up according to age—hoping the average group will number about thirty. The rationale is that it's easier for one teacher to build knowledge and skill levels with a group of similarly aged learners. That rationale makes sense if all the students are just passive learners. But don't we learn more ourselves when we teach others? The act of explaining something to someone else often clarifies the idea in our own mind. Indeed, research proves that the teacher-student learns more than the learner-student when they are paired for study.

In short, there's no reason to consider the varying ages in a family as a disadvantage in a joint venture such as a trip. When all appreciate the value and contribution of each, the total result will be greater than expected.

Time is a much more flexible element in family trips than in a school field trip. Usually, family trips last longer and have greater continuity than school-sponsored field trips. The family can set goals and make plans for a trip a whole year in advance. Furthermore, if the trip is successful, there is a greater chance for follow-up activities in the future. And, if somehow the trip was a flop, there's more opportunity to adjust the problem and hope for success next time. Best of all, there's greater stability among family members over a period of years.

In other words, a family trip isn't really just a one-shot deal. The trip builds on past family habits and raises ideas for future possibilities. As the world of family experience widens, everyone gets ideas that begin with, "Wouldn't it be neat if we. . .?"

To get the most from any trip, goals should be clearly understood. And it always helps, of course, if everyone involved knows the chosen goals. A well-conducted class field trip is the natural outgrowth of an interest developed in the classroom. First-graders learn about community helpers and then go visit the fire station. Sixth-graders learn about government and then go chat with the mayor or his staff. And when these children return to their classroom, they talk about what they've seen, heard, and done. The little ones draw pictures of their adventures with the fire truck; the older students write reports about the mayor's job. The same elements—goals, preparation, followup—influence the success of both family and school trips. So, when the family decides to take a trip to, say, Boston, first ask:

1. What are the basic goals and reasons for the trip? It's a business trip for Mom, but what's the point of dragging along the whole group? There must be some family goals, too. FAMILY GOAL 1: The family would like to spend more time together. FAMILY GOAL 2: Two sites would be interesting to visit—the Freedom Trail and the Boston harbor. The basic problem here is to ease the conflict between business and family goals. Does Mom want to attend a conference while the rest of the family plays tourist? Or does she want her time with the family to be spent visiting these sights? Will everyone be satisfied if the family time is limited to postmeeting dinners at the hotel and evening ex-

plorations of the city? These are issues that must be resolved to everyone's satisfaction. Otherwise the goals will be a source of confusion and conflict—and then Boston won't be any fun at all.

2. What kinds of preparation help to meet family goals? Remember that the class trips we examined were natural outgrowths of studies and discussions initiated by the teacher or by student interest. The "getting ready" time before a family trip can be shared at the dinner table. When the goals are openly discussed, everybody gets into the act with, "I want to see . . ." or "Why can't we. . .?" That can be a bit of a hassle sometimes, but it's a useful form of trip preparation.

Visual preparation is best for younger children. A picture of the Boston Commons or the old North Church taped to the refrigerator door can become a familiar sight and easily identifiable by even a four-year-old when confronted with the real thing. The abstract idea of Boston is too vague for a small child, but a picture of a specific landmark to watch for later—*that* focuses anticipation! Skyline or aerial views don't work, nor do abstract artistic travel folders. Mount one or two pictures cut from a brochure on the bathroom door, or make a collage for a bedroom wall. A child becomes so excited when he or she can identify the landmark on the spot. Don't be dismayed, however, if the child announces, "There's the church on our refrigerator!" Remembering the name at that point is less important. What is important is that the child realizes that a picture seen at home can be a *thing*—an object, a place—so many miles away.

Older children benefit from preparatory reading. Some encyclopedia articles are so attractively presented, with all sorts of pictures and maps and time lines, that a brief glance can reap a few interesting facts and ideas. This is no time for in-depth study. Rather, it's fun to speculate, "Gee, do you think we'll see this?" and "It says here that . . ." and "Did you know . . . ?"

Sometimes children enjoy an evening of listening to stories based on the place to be visited. The adventures of Paul Revere can give a new, personal view of old Boston. And later, when children stand beneath his statue and look up at the horse, the experience has greater meaning and provides a better background for understanding the man and the historical period.

Sudden spur-of-the-moment trips make this type of preparation next to impossible. It's hard enough just to get the clothes packed and count the noses in the back seat! But if the trip is to be of any length at all, gather up some pictures and stories to tell en route. Anything that tells about the destination helps pass the time profitably and builds anticipation.

3. What kinds of follow-up activities can a family do to build a clear, cohesive memory with meaning for all ages? Pictures, stories, shared "remember-whens" are all important. (Chapters 5 and 14 deal with specifics.) Were the family goals met? Was it a success? What could we do better next time? Are trips really worth the bother? What's your favorite memory?

Asking questions is important, and so is listening. What does your child say to his friends about the trip? Are his stories cohesive and meaningful? Is there joy in the retelling? Younger children tend to brag; teenagers shrug things off with an "OK."

These typical behaviors have to be acknowledged and parents can usually separate the reality of a child's feelings and memories from the child's version designed to share with friends.

Of course, the best test of the trip is to ask how willing everyone is to pick up and go again. What will be different the next time? The family group is essentially the same, but perhaps a little wiser and more experienced. Have the family goals shifted? "Perhaps this time we'll skip the sightseeing and just relax on the beach." Use the experiences from the last trip and build on them. "Here is the ocean that the British soldiers sailed across when they arrived in Boston. Remember Boston? Remember Paul Revere? He saw those soldiers coming!"

Remember, wherever children go, whatever they do, they are learning. You can make the most of family travel time to enrich and expand your children's world.

# 5

# Patterns for Learning and Remembering

Questions, questions, and more questions! Kids are full of them—all types of questions for all kinds of reasons—and not always for the purpose of learning something new.

The best questions are those which lead to further questions; one follows an investigative trail, never sure where the path may lead, but intrigued by the exploration. Educators have been encouraging this "Socratic" style of questioning in recent years. Inquiry is an active medium through which students learn both the content and the process of a discipline. The kinds of questions asked by learned people in different disciplines can guide even a novice in the general direction of meaningful inquiry. The key is to know what questions are being asked in each of the major discipline areas. Knowing these contributes to a meaningful whole—a paradigm—which guides disciplinary study.

Three obvious inquiry areas which pertain to a trip are social science, science, and math. Very simply, as the days of travel go by, children will come in contact with people, objects, and numerical values.

In general, social science is the study of human society. A number of separate disciplines are covered by the blanket term "social science." Two major disciplines which divide the study of humanity into time and space—history and geography—are so vast, they touch on many disciplines both in and out of social sciences.

History is the record of humanity's past. More accurately, it concerns those events which appear to be important to later generations. Historians study the time pattern of human events and frequently interpret these events according to some measure of success or failure. The historian asks "What happened?" "When?" "Who did it?" and "Why?" The last question can lead to an exploration of the variety of causes leading to an event, and beyond that, to the multitudinous effects upon individuals, groups, and nations.

If you apply these basic questions to some event discovered on a trip, you can guide a child through an investigation as broad or as narrow as the specific event, limited only by his own interest and the available information.

Geography is the study of the human relationship to the earth and its resources, and involves specific patterns of both natural and manufactured phenomena across the surface of the globe. History is time; geography is space. Geographers ask "What is where?" and "Why is it there?" Again, when "Why?" is asked, the search for cause-and-effect relationships is initiated.

These two areas are so wide and encompass so much information, a basic understanding of each has been considered essential by educators before a narrower study can be undertaken. Thus, for centuries history and geography have been the foundation of the school curriculum. They also act as a bridge between the sciences and the humanities. If one studies natural phenomena in temporal and spatial contexts, history and geography open the door to explorations in the natural sciences. For example, learning the geographic location of limestone and its historic use in architecture may open an interest in geology. Studying human behavior patterns in particular times and places serves as historical and geographical introduction to other social sciences. Learning the history of settlement patterns in the United States might lead to discussion about psychological and sociological factors involved in the decision to migrate.

A family trip is a natural springboard for the historian's and geographer's questions. Such questions, from the mouths of children, are very valuable in their personal understanding of the world. Remembering Piaget's explanation of children's developmental stages, these questions have specific utility for children searching for patterns of reality.

Reality is discovered and organized in patterns. These patterns are very useful to us. They help us to comprehend a situation and to remember separate pieces or facts which form the pattern. Often, common patterns can be printed for guidance or clarity. Road maps are a perfect example. Roads are laid out in patterns which reflect paths of human activity. The map reveals obvious and subtle patterns; concrete patterns suggest abstract patterns and cause-and-effect relationships. Some roads bend to avoid mountains, others come together, revealing that people have, in times past, selected a site for settlement. How much your child can comprehend from, say, map patterns depends on his achieved developmental level. A parent can help learning by arranging fragments of knowledge in recognizable patterns according to: (1) the nature of the phenomenon and the questions which pertain to it, and (2) the child's developmental level.

Patterns form the web or the structure of our knowledge. They are also part of the method by which we obtain further knowledge: the scientific method. The word "science" was used by the Romans to mean "knowledge." Today we use it to refer to a particular branch of knowledge, the natural sciences. When we think of science, we usually think of chemistry, botany, geology, zoology, and physics. Each of these areas are investigated by way of the scientific method. It may sound formal and austere, but it's basically a somewhat refined trial-and-error process. John Dewey first applied the method to children's learning environments and it is still used in many formal and informal school situations.

The first step of the scientific method is to define the problem. What are we looking for? What problem are we trying to solve? Sounds simple enough until you consider how frequently we all run around in circles looking for answers to problems we've not yet recognized. A young child picks up a stick and bangs away at the nearest tree. What's he trying to find out? Will the tree fall? Will the stick break? Or, what kind of a noise will it make? Will those kids over there become curious and join in the play? The tree doesn't present a problem *per se;* the child's approach to the tree raises questions in his or her mind. Identifying the problem, stating it, and defining it are all ways adults can develop the questions raised by a child's curiosity. Recognizing that a problem exists, that it may arise from mere curiosity or from actual need is the first step. But that first step is only partially taken or may lead straight to frustration if the problem is misunderstood or stated improperly.

Problems may surface as broad complaints. A strange dish was set before John in a restaurant and he reacted with,

"Mommy, I don't like this food . . . it's bad."

"What's the matter with it?"

"I just don't like it."

The problem of what's wrong with the food, stated so generally, can lead directly to frustration. Be more specific. What does the child expect the food to be? The problem can then be restated as "What makes this food different from what I like?"

The second step is suggesting a hypothesis or a guess. With a little poking about with the fork, can your child come up with some reasons why he doesn't like this dish? Maybe it has different ingredients than those used in Mom's kitchen. Maybe the food is actually bad. Maybe it's a dish he hasn't had before. Each hypothesis should be tested—that's the next step. And finally a solution

42

to the problem is found. Of course, I didn't say he'd eat what's on his plate—but now he has a more precise reason for not liking the meal!

The scientific method can be applied to problems with far more substance than this example, with far more valuable results. Kids are trial-and-error people. The only guidance they need is for someone to state the problem and help isolate several hypotheses which can be tested in a logical manner. While not all questions can be answered in this manner, the pattern of organized thought is invaluable in many trip situations.

Mathematics is another useful discipline in trip-related investigations. Math is the reduction of phenomena to numbers. The mathematician asks "How many?" The relationship between numbers revealed through mathematical processes can tell us about the size, amount, structure, properties, and monetary value of a phenomenon. (Again, your child can see relationships between quantities only insofar as his developmental level allows him.)

Sociology is the study of human social behavior. It focuses on relations between groups of people, the individuals who compose groups, and patterns of group living. Sociologists ask "How are people grouped?" and "What effects do groups have on each other and on individuals?"

The roles that individuals play are related to the values and beliefs of the particular group to which they belong. A trip offers opportunities to meet a variety of people, and these contacts can teach children how "those other people" live. We usually measure differences between people and people's behavior according to our own personal yardsticks. A sociologist looks for causes and effects, and doesn't label behavior as "good" or "bad." Since a brief meeting is unlikely to have a lasting effect upon a child, a trip is a safe time to allow some supervised mixing with people that your family may not wish to choose as permanent friends. Take a brief step into another person's world for a look around and a chance later for family discussion about what makes other people tick. Remind children that others are not "better" or "worse," only "different." Why bother to see different lands if we can't meet the different people who make those lands their home? And beyond meeting them, there is the interesting opportunity to consider others' roles within their own social groups.

Other social sciences may prove relevant to your trip objectives depending on your plans. A trip to the state or national capital? Political science! A visit to a museum or an Indian burial mound? Anthropology! A tour through a factory or a bank? Economics!

Perhaps family interest is geared to the natural sciences. Then, geographic exploration can lead to a comparison of plants in different areas (botany) or animals (zoology). The rocks that appear so different in shape and color can launch a geological investigation.

One final word. Children needn't spend time learning facts during a trip—that's not the point at all. Far more valuable is the time spent asking questions which lead to more questions. The remaining chapters in this book are filled with specific suggestions for activities which are intended to develop questioning and checking ability in children at different levels of development.

# 6

# Follow the Map

Geography is something to see, to touch, and even to taste. It's easier to get hold of than history. History has left behind remnants to touch, but the memories symbolized by the objects are elusive to young minds. Geography is concrete; history is abstract. So begin with the land and the people. The stories of their past will come later.

Maps are the tools of geographers, and they can be used to help a child understand the land he will see, is seeing, or has seen. Maps are useful at all stages of the trip: planning, traveling, and remembering. All kinds of speciality maps are available, which add more to a child's understanding of the family trip. Local gas stations, chambers of commerce, and state tourism bureaus furnish road maps. Maps can be obtained through mail request if the trip is planned at least six weeks in advance.

Besides the roads between home and the destination, what can be added to a child's store of useful information by a map? In the following pages, we'll examine ways of using ordinary road maps for learning about landforms, population centers, political divisions, points of interest, and of course, mileage. We'll also consider other types of maps and how they can guide investigation.

For a very young child, a map can be reassuring. Even though we've never been there before, we can locate a strange new place by following the directions on this piece of paper called a map. The shapes and colors of the road signs and the route numbers are the same on the map as those found along the highway. Pointing out these similarities shows the child that guideposts are clear all along his way between home and the unknown.

Remember that younger children, below the age of ten, will have difficulty in adjusting between maps of different scale. The easiest method is to use only one ROAD MAP which covers the entire trip area. Even though it may take a long time to cross even a small portion of the map on a coast-to-coast tour, the younger child can profit more from continually referring to one clear map, than from a variety of differently scaled maps. If another map of a small area is used, be sure to circle (in GREASE PENCIL, CRAYON, or FELT-TIP MARKER) the corresponding area on the larger basic map which the child is using for the entire trip.

An interesting project for young children involves learning to identify road signs on maps, so that they can recognize these signs on the highways. Examine a map of your intended routes.

Some highways are labeled as county or state roads. Others are federal routes, designated by two differently shaped shields—one for the older U.S. highways, the other for the new interstates. Point out these highway route numbers as they appear on the map and suggest that they be drawn larger on PAPER. Each route sign, complete with number, should be drawn about four-by-five inches. It will be easier for younger children to draw if you cut out the basic shape from a piece of CARDBOARD and allow them to create their numbered route signs by tracing around the pattern.

The completed signs should be placed in a pile and taken along on the trip. Help children ages four to seven to place the signs in order ahead of time. "If we leave our town on this road, which highway number should we look for first? Let's place that sign on top of the pile. And then what sign should we look for? That sign should be second in the pile. . . ." During the trip, the child can use the pile to answer his own question, "Where are we *now*?" Each prepared sign refers to the road signs and the routes on the map.

The color of route signs doesn't appear on most road maps. If you want the child to color the signs ahead of time in order to help him locate the real ones, you'll have to tell him the colors. Or take along a box of CRAYONS and let him color the signs according to what he sees from his car window. Older children don't need such large signs, but smaller ones can be shuffled and placed in order by the child according to his observations during the trip.

Another activity for the older child requires a BLANK, OUTLINED MAP of the area to be traveled, a

COMPASS, and the ROUTE SIGNS. For example, suppose the trip is from Washington, D.C. to New York City. The blank map should outline all of the states through which you plan to travel: Maryland, Delaware, New Jersey, and New York. In a corner of the map, indicate the compass directions. By observing his compass and the road signs along the way, the child can create a map en route. Later he can compare his map with a road map to see just how close he came to the real location of the Delaware Memorial Bridge and the interstate routes you followed. Don't expect a high degree of accuracy. The child is merely making some fun guesses while learning to use two tools of travelers: the compass and road signs.

Here's another method of using route signs with maps for a widespread age group. Mount a small ROAD MAP in the center of a piece of CARDBOARD, which could double as a lapboard for backseat crayoners. Surround the map with samples of the route signs you will be following. Cover the board with HEAVY PLASTIC WRAP. On the plastic, cover the road signs that appear on the road map beneath it, leaving side roads and place names still visible. Small pieces of MASKING TAPE over the route numbers will do the trick. As the child travels and identifies the route, he can use a GREASE PENCIL to draw an arrow from the identified sign to its map location. To check his answer, he can peel off the covering you used to hide the map signs (See Figure 6.1).

The beginning and the end of a trip are especially important to a small child. Have him place his fingers at the beginning and the end of a day's planned route. If the line between isn't straight, a

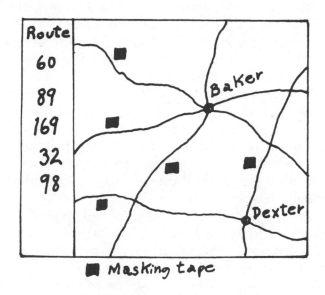

Figure 6.1. Make a map for back-seat drivers

few good questions might be raised. What natural or manmade obstruction forces the road to bend? Any age child can make some guesses to be checked out along the way. Younger children can identify such water barriers as rivers and lakes as they appear on the map.

While a mountain barrier is not always easy to see on an ordinary road map, the effects of mountains can be seen by the curves in the roads. It's interesting to compare the contour road pattern along the valleys of Pennsylvania with the straight grid road pattern of flat Iowa. Such contrasts are important to point out to young children who have difficulty picturing any pattern other than the one before their eyes at the moment.

A body of water or a mountain which changes

the direction of a youngster's travel can introduce some abstract thoughts in response to the question, "Why don't they just build a bridge across the water right here?" or "Why don't they just put a tunnel through the mountain?"

Bridge or tunnel construction implies money —more money than "they" (we taxpayers) spend to build highways to cross flat land. The longer the construction, the more money it takes. The more recent the construction, the more technical knowledge available. (Chapters 8 and 11 will expand on this point.)

A long river or bay is crossed at key points. How is the site for bridge construction chosen? First, of course, the site must not be too difficult for the level of technological development. The other basic considerations are suggested by a road map: Who will use the bridge? Where are they coming from? Where are they going? Why?

Show a young child the map and let him put his finger on the line that represents the bridge. What's on either side? How far would people have to travel if the bridge weren't there? Clear examples of saved travel distance are the Mackinac Bridge in Michigan and the Chesapeake Bay Bridge and Tunnel in Virginia. Let the child trace his finger around the coastline or across other available bridges so he can get a concrete idea of the distance saved by the bridge he will cross.

Then take a look at the mapped road that crossed the bridge. Does it connect two towns or cities? Does it connect parts of a city separated by water? Does it connect a city with suburbs on the other shore? Is it part of an interstate system? On some shores, it's possible to see a pattern of several

roads coming together in order to cross the connecting link: the bridge across the water barrier.

Tunnels are found less frequently since it is
easier for modern earthmoving equipment to
knock over a hill than to burrow through it. Much
of what has been said about bridge patterns on a
map is also true of tunnels.

We have already discussed the different
shapes of country, state and federal road signs.
The road map uses different colors to mark different levels of road quality. Younger children should
be given an explanation of the colors and older
children should be introduced to the map key or
legend which provides the information for them.
Whether or not they have used map keys before, a
trip is an excellent time to become familiar with
the helpful knowledge they provide.

In relation to water and mountain barriers, it's
interesting to note that the straighter lines on the
road map are the new, brightly colored interstates.
They may be boring to travel, but they get you
where you're going in the shortest possible time
and distance. How is it that the other roads turn
and twist to avoid barriers while nothing appears
to interfere with the straightness of an interstate?
The older child might consider the controversy behind these two patterns. Discuss the economy and
convenience of an interstate versus the ecological
disturbance it causes. The child can compare the
mileage of older roads with the interstates and
count the number of congested areas which would
slow thru-traffic. He should also examine the land
through which the interstate travels. Is it farmland? Wilderness? Suburbs? Older children can
compute estimates of the land area involved in the

highway construction. How many acres or miles of farmland and/or wilderness is devoted to the highway? There aren't any single "right" answers to problems of interstate construction. Nevertheless, discussion encourages abstract thought and awareness of decisions required by taxpayers and consumers. It's also an interesting way to clarify family and personal values and, in so doing, learn more about each other. Remember that clarifying is an activity best carried out in an atmosphere of mutual acceptance.

The road map will show children other interesting patterns, such as the shape of an octopus as roads reach out from an urban area to ease flow of traffic. The key will aid the older child in determining the population of urban areas, but even the younger child will be able to compare the size of the different urban spreads. Larger areas usually have more connecting arteries. Ask: "Why do more people need more roads? What are all the roads used for?" The curiosity raised by a map can make a trip more exciting.

Some cities have tried to solve their traffic problems with encircling rings or beltways which also make interesting map patterns. Beltways appear to take thru-traffic out of its way. A trip involving in-city and around-city travel provides an interesting opportunity for time and mileage comparisons by older children. Recorded data will probably confirm the conveniences of the beltway for the interstate traveler, but is that the only purpose of such highways? Children's observation of increased traffic volume near urban areas ought to give some clue to the major purpose of roads which circle the óutskirts, that is, alleviating inner city congestion.

If you travel on roads other than interstates, children may observe abrupt differences in construction material used for the road, and changes in road width or shoulder construction. Usually these sharp, sudden changes are accompanied by signs at the side of the road announcing the boundary of a separate political unit, e.g., a different county or state. Most road maps indicate state and county boundaries, unless the travel distance is quite lengthy. When a boundary is crossed, an older child may consult the map for the political information. Where is the capital or seat of government? If the road you've been traveling passes through that city, then all ages will want to be on the lookout for the courthouse or state capitol building. The age and style of these buildings make for interesting comparisons.

Maps have other interesting details and older children can find their symbols in the key. Frequently, special roads are marked because of their historic significance. The Great River Road follows the route of the Mississippi; the Natchez Trace was an important eighteenth century commercial and military route; the Lewis and Clark Trail marks the route of their explorations. Road maps often note the significance of these routes and the locations of special monuments along the way. Check the key on your road map for other items that can arouse interest in the view beyond the window.

Buses travel along highways routed by road maps. Airline and train travel are a different matter. Train tracks are drawn on some road maps, which makes them usable in some of the same ways described earlier. Older children can compute miles in distance and in time to compare plane, train, and car travel. Cost per mile can also be figured by older children in order to compare cost-efficiency for auto, plane, and train travelers. Younger children might wonder: "Why are we traveling by train or plane and leaving the car at home? What are some of the good things about this kind of travel?"

Most commercial airplanes provide air route maps which show the arc of flight over a realistic graphic illustration of the landforms—an interesting contrast with a road map. Even a young child can see the geographic barriers that are avoided by taking to the sky.

But why are the flight paths between distant points drawn in arcs? Remember that the map may be flat but the earth is round. An arc is a straight line over a curved surface. Some airline maps compensate for that confusion by drawing the flight paths in straight lines, but the land beneath is distorted in shape. Older children can compare these two types of maps as two different ways to tell the same story.

Not all maps tell how to get to a place by either land or air. Some are visual aids supplying different sorts of information, such as population maps, land use maps, vegetation maps, and climate and rainfall maps. The type most often included in tourist packets is a pictorial map of local attractions. Young children delight in circling (or coloring or clipping) scenes which they will visit. Sometimes arrows can be added indicating the direction of travel.

Older children with a real interest in maps can use several types to prepare for a visit to a new area. Suggest they write a short description, based on map information, of what they expect to find when they arrive. These are so interesting to reread after a day or two in the area. It's even more enlightening if several children record their expectations for later comparison. When what they expected differs from what they see, most children stop and look closer. The result is an improvement of observation and comparison skills.

Let maps raise as many questions as possible. Some can be answered by considering other facts revealed by the map and others are better answered by observing the scene when you arrive. Other questions are best answered by books once the trip is only a pleasant memory. When a map raises questions for a child, it is more than a guide; it is a springboard for inquiry.

# 7

# Make a Time Line

"Tomorrow when we saw those Indians, you said we were going to a rodeo today."

"Mary, I think you are a bit confused."

Yesterday, today, and tomorrow are very confusing concepts to small children. The idea that a trip is going to take a week of travel has little reality for a small one who asks every ten minutes, "Are we there yet?"

This is a situation when the historian's questions have special relevance. Helping to sort out questions of time in a child's mind enables an adult to divert monotonous "childish" questioning into patterns of discovery for everyone. The new and different focus of the child's questioning from the back seat may also help to preserve sanity in the front seat! For instance, you could turn the question "How old is that?" into a discussion of the relativity of time.

Depending upon one's perspective, the word *old* has a variety of meanings. Obviously, it refers to a time which has passed. But it's a vague label, and doesn't specify exact age. An old house in Pratt, Kansas appears young when compared to an old house in Plymouth, Massachusetts. And neither of them is considered very old by tourists strolling through the Tower of London or the ruins of the Parthenon. Children integrate the relative age of each of these examples within the framework of their own experience with old things—like last year's bicycle and yesterday's lollipop. Separate distinctions rarely exist in a child's thinking, particularly in the lower developmental stages.

The word *old* is frequently value-laden. Individual and social tastes often determine whether something old is worthwhile or useless. The same old china plate may be treated quite differently by three people. The first notes that it doesn't match her china set and since it's been around for awhile, it's old, it's junk, and out it goes! The second might display the same china plate in a prominent place because it's an old and valuable antique. The last might lovingly use the china plate because it's old and familiar; it brings back memories of her grandmother.

Most children are familiar with the first attitude toward something old. We live in a throwaway, disposable era of paper and plastics. "Old" usually means "throw it out!" Unfortunately this attitude is sometimes extended to our values about people. The young are thought to be strong, good, and beautiful; the old, wrinkled, worn, and unlovely. Frequently, older folk are the repository of valuable memories and practical advice. Unfortunately, it's a rare twentieth-century child who has the opportunity to find out firsthand about the older generation. (See Chapter 8 for ideas in contacting older folk.)

The first step to take in dealing with your child's understanding of time is to find out what your child thinks about the term *old*.

"What is old? Can you find something around you that's old? Watch through the window as we go."

"Well, there's an old house. See, it doesn't have any paint."

Both the choice and the stated reason are important.

"If the house were freshly painted, would it still *look* old? Would it still *be* old? What's the difference between looking old and being old?"

Frequently, a child's response to this line of questioning reveals a negative attitude toward old things, meaning things that are used up or are in bad condition. At this point you might ask the child to consider relative ages. "Is that house older than the tree in the yard? Older than that other house down the street? Older than you? Older than me? Older than Grandma?"

Other questions highlight the value of saving something old. Sometime, someone, somewhere decided that those historic buildings and artifacts which are now preserved should be declared "old and valuable." Why did someone take the time and interest to bother with such an idea? And if something old is valuable, why aren't all old things considered valuable? Who decides and why?

Obviously, there aren't any right answers to these questions of value. What is important to one person may have no value at all to another. But it is important that your child speculate on possible reasons why some old things have been preserved and displayed. Museums are filled with items related in one way or another to some historic person or event. Here is a bullet fired at Gettysburg; there is a tavern where General Washington once stopped for rest. Ask why these things have value or importance for those who exhibit or view them.

Sometimes objects or structures are chosen for preservation because they tell a story of the past. And the story makes more sense because we have preserved this bit of visual evidence.

"This is the kind of wagon which took the settlers west to California."

"This is the kind of home the Indians built."

"This is the type of kitchen equipment colonial women used."

Each article tells a story of a struggle for existence and the inventive nature of those who succeeded. Interestingly enough, modern campers, with all the conveniences available to them, could find a number of creative ideas among the hearthside implements used by New England settlers. Raise other questions for your child: Can something old continue to be used? Or, after long disuse, can something be used again?

A quick example, appreciated by older children, is to note the recycling of clothing styles and music. You might ask, "What makes people want to return for another look at something old?" Again, there really isn't any right answer. Psychologists tell us that we tend to retreat to the familiar for security. During the fifties, it was popular to recreate the twenties and during the seventies, there appeared a revival of the styles and language of the fifties. It's fun to look back over fond memories and somehow, separated by time from current pressures, those former periods seem funnier and easier than now.

More concrete examples, useful for very young children, are found all along the highways. An old building is left abandoned because of its age. But in other places, the same type of building is still a useful place because someone has deemed it worth saving.

Remember the old-fashioned gas station? Sometimes built of brick, sometimes of wood, it was usually a square, two-story structure with pillars out front to support the extended roof. Cars drove under the roof to reach the single gas pump. The attendant's family usually had an apartment on the second floor. Most of those old-style gas stations have been torn down and replaced by modern facilities that can accommodate more customers more quickly. Now and then, particularly in the country, these stations stand abandoned and overgrown with weeds. You may get a rare glimpse of an old station still operating.

Ask the children to consider these relics of another era. Compare the old-fashioned station with the new. What's the difference? Could those smaller stations with more limited facilities and upstairs living quarters give some clues to the differences in people's lives then and now? Older children will probably remember pictures of cars and clothing styles from the era of early motoring.

Occasionally, it's possible to find one of these stations serving a new purpose. Some have been turned into homes, but most have been converted into other roadside businesses. The children might consider the question, "What makes that old building usable for this new business and yet unsuitable as a gas station?" Clues they might pick up are: (1) its good location; (2) its good condition; (3) its size and shape; and (4) it's sometimes cheaper to paint and clean a building than it is to tear it down and build another.

These examples point out some methods of determining your child's thinking when the word *old* is used. Having uncovered the child's point of view, you may begin aiding him or her to untangle confusing questions of chronology, such as "Which came first?"

All children have trouble assigning historical periods to objects on display or events commemorated by some monument. A time line is a graphic measure of time which minimizes their confusion. For very young children, a time line which goes beyond their years is of little value, but a four-year-old can make and illustrate his own time line of events during the trip. The four-year-old "preoperational" child *does* understand concepts of past and future, but, since children of that age believe things follow their rules, sequences of events may be difficult for them to grasp. There's no point in dealing with the remote past or the distant future in specific terms. The relative age of objects and their value can be explored, but the discrete difference between a battle fought in 1863 and one in 1777 just won't be comprehended by a four-year-old.

What is important to the preschooler is, "What did I do today and what will I do tomorrow?" It's fun to draw pictures of the most exciting thing that happened that day. Large productions can be expressive, but for ease in travel the child should be given a SMALL PAD OF PAPER. Each day have the child draw a picture of the day's events. To keep the events in sequence, number the pictures and attach them with MASKING TAPE to the back of the front seat. That works best if the child is the lone occupant of the back seat; otherwise there's too much paper and too little room.

Another alternative is to PASTE the separate pictures in chronological order from left to right on a ROLL OF SHELF PAPER which can be rolled up daily and stored in a box. Obviously, you won't need a whole roll for this. A piece five to ten feet long should be all you need. A child who is learning the sequence of numbers will enjoy applying them to his pictures of important events.

That's a key point—focus on the events which appear important to the child. It is, after all, *his* or *her* experience and this perception will undoubtedly be quite different from your own. Seeing the Washington Monument may be far less important to a four-year-old than feeding the squirrel on the grounds near the base of the monument. Since understanding a time-sequence of events is the purpose of the exercise, let the child determine the importance of an event from his own viewpoint.

The roll of shelf paper may be prepared ahead of time. With a yardstick, draw a line along the length of the center of the paper. Then draw lines across it at regular intervals, dividing the paper into a number of spaces equal to the days of the trip. The horizontal line is the time line (see Figure 7.1).

The older child can fill in the spaces of the

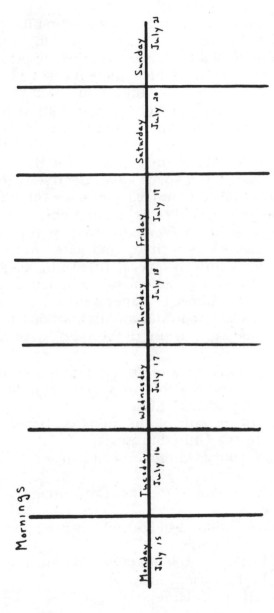

Mornings

Monday July 15　Tuesday July 16　Wednesday July 17　Thursday July 18　Friday July 19　Saturday July 20　Sunday July 21

Afternoons

Figure 7.1.　Time line for travel

63

day's trip with postcards, news clippings, and other collected paper souvenirs. Older children are also capable of placing historic periods in perspective, using a time line which encompasses a longer time period, beyond the limitations of their day-to-day experience. They can identify a phenomenon in relation to its time of origin or its period of significance. A child between seven and eleven, in the "concrete operations" stage, can deal with concepts of time and space very effectively. Being in a different place in order to see something from another time is conceivable to older children, and they are able to place events in proper perspective. Difficulty arises when times and dates from several different events in several different places pile up during a journey and cause confusion. A time line drawn on a sheet of paper showing the time periods they will encounter at various stops during the trip can be most useful to the youngsters along the way.

For example, on a relatively small peninsula in Virginia, it is possible to view the following places in one whirlwind day:

1. Jamestown, site of the first English settlement in the United States;
2. Williamsburg, a colonial town of a later period;
3. Yorktown, site of the last Revolutionary War battle;
4. Kicotan Indian Village, which predated English settlements;
5. the Mariners Museum collection encompassing all of nautical history;
6. the harbor of Hampton Roads, site of the

Civil War battle between the *Monitor* and the *Merrimack*; and

7. Aerospace Park, displaying jets, rockets, and missiles.

The timespan represented here is well over three hundred years and extends much longer if you include all the exhibits in the Mariners Museum. How confusing for a child, even if the sightseeing is more sensibly spread over several days.

Prepare a blank time line before leaving home. The child can then fill in what he sees and learns as he travels (see Figure 7.2). The finished product probably won't look like the example given because what your children choose to place on their time lines will be based on their own interests, their individual investigations and the artifacts available for their observations. A time line can also be an attractive decoration. Small pictures, hand-drawn or cut from tourist folders and restaurant place mats, can add to the meaning of a creative time line. If the trip will cover prehistoric geological phenomena as well as more recent historical occurrences, it may be wise to use separate sheets of paper, then place them in proper sequence. If only one sheet were used, and each time segment were given an equal space on the time line, the segment on the Civil War, for example, would be so small as to be completely unreadable in comparison to the empty eons of the prehistoric periods.

Time lines can be extremely helpful when visiting sites related to a specific person or event. For example, if your trip follows the Lincoln Trail from Kentucky to Illinois, limit the time line to the

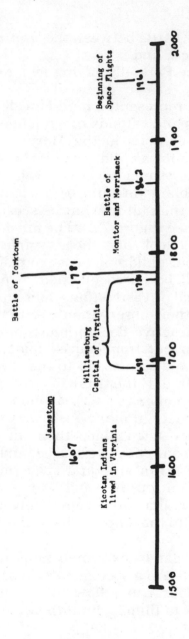

Figure 7.2. Completed time line

length of Lincoln's life and let the child fill in important dates and the names of the places Lincoln lived during his years in these states.

A young teenager, having entered the "formal operations" level, can deal very comprehensively with time line data. A trip to the Carolinas may result in a visit to Kitty Hawk and a time line about the development of human flight. A later trip to the Minnesota home of Lindbergh would supply data for a complementary time line. Guesses can then be made about the possible effect of the events at Kitty Hawk on the Lindbergh child born the year before the Wrights' first success. Beyond that, your teenager might make some hypotheses on the effect of space explorations on his own generation.

Another example of comparative analysis of time lines would be the use of a geological time line as supportive data for the success or failure of given industries in the same area at a later time period. The opening of coal mines, the building of a steel plant, and the development of farmland are all dependent for their success on the geologic history of their sites.

Time lines are such useful tools, both when they are created and for later clarification of possible cause-and-effect relationships. Making a graphic display of a fact in time makes it possible for children to deal with elusive abstractions in a concrete manner.

# 8

# Stop, Look, and Listen

A map is just a page of clues which gives a child some ideas about where to look and what to ask. A time line just classifies events chronologically. Both are patterns for arranging ideas—one by space, the other by time. But the essential ingredient of learning lies in the mind of the child, in his or her curiosity.

A basic educational argument has grown over the years, fed in part by the theories mentioned in Chapter 3. Should curriculum designers choose and impose "important" information upon schoolchildren, or should children determine what are important problems worth solving? These philosophies are termed *teacher-centered* vs. *child-centered* education. Which is best? No one is *really* sure; hence the controversy continues.

However, there's enough evidence on hand to verify the logical assumption that if a kid is interested in what he's doing, he'll learn more about it, no matter what it is—football strategy, fort building, or even something "important" like history. Child-centered education promotes enthusiastic involvement which stems from motivation within the child.

What does this mean for parents interested in educating their children through travel? Should the kid run the show? Should he be the one to call the shots? That would be a common mistake in this black or white, either/or world of ours. Child-centered education becomes child tyranny under that set of rules. But the level of children's involvement in planning and decision making is directly related to their level of interest in the undertaking itself. If your child knows that part of each vacation day will be devoted to his interests, then his curiosity will certainly be heightened.

The words *look* and *listen* in this chapter's title refer to observation skills that need to be sharpened in order to raise your child's curiosity about new environments. But the stop sign is also an essential factor. To be an effective looker and listener with your child, it is necessary to stop and consider his point of view. This is the heart of the child-centered educational philosophy, which says, after John Dewey: Stop and consider the interests of your child; help him look and listen to things which will help him learn.

So what should we look at? What will raise a child's curiosity? Almost anything, especially if enthusiasm is built into the package. A monotone lecture from Father behind the wheel is straight out of the teacher-centered philosophy. What we're looking for are questions—enthusiastic questions—

from children *and* adults. Behind our questions we are saying: life is a curious thing and there's so much to wonder about! Learning is a lifelong process—and it's fun.

So, let's begin to look. There's a world beyond the car windows, but at 55 mph all we see is a passing glance. However, the lay of the land (while seemingly the same for miles) gives clues about its geological history and geographical value.

Superhighways have advantages and disadvantages for observing landforms. These roads smooth out the path of travel so that it is possible to travel on the same plane without any conscious thought of hills, plateaus, or valleys. It is only when we increase the accelerator on an uphill climb that we realize a change in the land about us. It takes a special brand of observation to detect different landforms when riding on an interstate. One interesting thing to look for is a "road cut," a slice through the earth made by large highway construction machinery in order to smooth the way for the road. Road cuts are worth a stop for a closer look, but much can be observed by even a quick glance.

Is the exposed rock in blocks or layers? The difference between the two gives evidence of their origin. Layers of rock have been laid down, one upon another, often on the bottom of an ancient sea. Large blocks of rock were formed by the extreme heat and pressure of the lower regions of the earth's crust. The blocks pictured in Figure 8.1 are quartzite, a metamorphic rock; its structure is quite different from the sedimentary layers in Figure 8.2.

Figure 8.1. Quartzite rock

Figure 8.2. Sedimentary rock layers

71

This is a sketchy description of geological processes, but unless your child is really curious about these things, you won't need much more explanation. It only takes a brief glance to identify sedimentary layers. The nature of the layering can give you some clue as to how the hill was formed thousands of years before.

Ask the children to watch for layers that bend, to wonder about forces strong enough to bend and twist the earth.

Internal earthmoving forces formed hills and mountains through folding and block uplifting processes. Even though erosion may have leveled the area long since, the original signs of folding are visible in the bent layers of road cuts. In the northern Midwestern states, north and south roads tend to roll and cut through small east-west hills. These hills (or *moraines*) and the fertile till plains between them are ancient remnants of the presence of continental glaciers that covered the area many thousands of years ago. The straight highways curve only when circuiting a lake whose bed was scraped out of the earth by a glacier long ago. Help your child imagine the powerful forces that build a hill or a mountain, and the quiet, patient, erosive forces that tear it down. Emphasize the long periods of time involved. Children tend to believe such things could happen instantly, somewhat like a televised cartoon!

Has the earth finished all its building and eroding processes? This type of question can direct a child's thinking toward constant change taking place in what appears to be a calm and quiet world. Look for forces in action to provide clues to processes of change. One of the most obvious is a river and its cutting and carrying effect on the land. Even large boulders are subject to flood waters as they tear away the supporting soil beneath (Figure 8.3).

When approaching a large river, look at the drainage patterns' effect on the land. It is a silent tale of the forces of water. A placid river in summer can be a rush of angry water in the throes of spring floods. Point out the narrow gorges carved by flowing water and the fertile flat flood plains which have benefited, over time, from high water flowing over them and depositing rich silt. Oxbow lakes (actually old bends in the river, now separated from the river) can help a child visualize the forces which can change the entire course of a river.

Storms also change land forms; high winds blow the soil particles about, and strong tides shift

Figure 8.3. Rushing flood waters cut through the land

the sands of coastal beaches. Often, it's easier for a child to notice buildings damaged by storms than to see changes in the land (Figure 8.4).

"Wow! Look at what the hurricane did to the house!"

"If a storm can do that to a house, look around and see if you can tell what it did to the land." The attention attracted by a disaster can be directed to a wider area of investigation.

The way the land lies has an effect on the direction roads take. "Why are there so many curves in the hills? Remember how straight the road was across the plains? Why should this be?" Even an older child constructing a model landform will unrealistically build roads going straight up steep slopes unless he has previously noticed how winding roads which follow the contour of the land decrease the steepness of the grade.

As you drive along a narrow valley bottom, you may find the highway, the telephone lines, a railroad track, and a river following parallel routes. Ask, "Why are all the routes so close together?" This

Figure 8.4.   A house leveled by hurricane winds

is an example of a situation which is accepted as obvious by adults. But asking questions helps a child recognize relationships between different phenomena. In this case, the child will see the effect of a landform which is a narrow passage for human transportation and communication.

Some tourist attractions capitalize on scenery. Unique landforms have been preserved and inspire awe in the tourists who visit them yearly. The most familiar examples are the Grand Canyon, the Old Faithful geyser, and the deserts of the Southwest. Recently, environmental movements have increased this audience and your children are probably well aware of reasons for preserving these unique forms of nature. It is fun to see such awesome sights from various angles and sometimes local promoters provide the means. It is possible to see Niagara Falls from a helicopter, a boat, a tower, and from a tunnel behind the falls. It's a little too hectic and expensive to take all the tours of all the possible viewpoints. A few moments of quiet analysis before viewing the natural phenomenon, in order to make a family plan of action, will insure greater satisfaction for all members of the group. In the Wisconsin Dells, you can take several boat rides which travel among the rock formations or take a vehicle called a "Duck" that goes overland and through water. In the Everglades you could take an air boat or a canoe. Consider three things when planning an activity: (1) How long are your children's attention spans, and how does that compare to trip lengths of different vehicles? (2) Will this trip provide a special or unique viewpoint? (3) Is that viewpoint worth the cost?

Population patterns can encourage curiosity

through inquiry. The first and most obvious questions to ask are: "Why do people choose to live here? What do they do for work?" You'll find clear answers in large industrial districts. A cluster of a few buildings at a crossroads is often a service center for vast farmlands. Larger cities have complicated commercial and industrial networks which are less easily analyzed by young minds. Even without stopping the car, children can note the following at the fringes of large cities:

- industrial areas devoted to warehouses, manufacturing plants, truck depots, and railroad yards;
- increased traffic flow on the highway you are traveling, and an increased number of intersections or cloverleaves;
- change in the types of traffic. Large semi-trailer trucks that dominate cross-country highways now compete for space with small local vans.

Road facilities themselves are worth observing. Road surfaces, access routes, and rest stops provide clues as to the local or state level of economy and zoning. Local highways are made from local materials. County road surfaces sometimes change abruptly, depending on the type of gravel locally available. Compare road shoulder gravels changing from county to county.

No driver likes to be routed through construction sites, but your back seat crew may be delighted. Since you're going to be delayed anyway, investigate how the roads are built. Note that bridge (and tunnel) construction changes according to the period and level of technical development at the time that it was built (see Figure 8.5).

**Figure 8.5.** Different types of bridge construction

If you anticipate crossing a bridge on your trip, your child might benefit by reading about bridge types in an illustrated encyclopedia. New advances represented by the Mackinac Bridge and the Chesapeake Bay Bridge and Tunnel are especially interesting when contrasted with older covered bridges found in New England and Pennsylvania.

Be sure to leave room in your trip schedule for serendipity. A spur-of-the-moment surprise exploration can brighten any long day of travel. Unbelievably, one gas station located in the middle of the flat Midwestern plains featured an elephant! A crazy, fun, model elephant strong enough to climb and poke and examine (see Figure 8.6).

For children, the very best objects to explore are the touchable kind. If seven-year-old John can spend some time behind the wheel of an antique

Figure 8.6.  A serendipitous elephant in the Midwest

fire engine, manipulating the gears and levers, his imagination can soar (Figure 8.7). It's so much better than standing and looking with hands in pockets. Some museums like the Children's Museum in Boston and the Museum of Science and Industry in Chicago have begun to specialize in this type of "hands-on" exhibit. Their rooms are filled with real-life objects to handle, examine, and manipulate.

Of course, such exhibits aren't always available. But, even if your child is barred from touching by a restrictive fence, there is still value in thinking with him or her, "I wonder what it would be like to drive that train? Look how big it is compared to us!" Some exhibits are so striking, such as the tiger at the Smithsonian National Museum of Natural History in Washington, D.C., that children

Figure 8.7.  John explores an antique fire engine

often listen to the voice in the earphones for longer than usual. (See Figures 8.8 and 8.9.)

There's an attitudinal difference between a serendipitous road experience and a planned visit to a museum. The roadside pause is a break in a monotonous drive. With a limited number of items to view or touch, interest can be focused on one or two ideas. On the other hand, a museum is a kaleidoscope of experiences and you might find yourself saying, "To make this trip worthwhile, we're going to see them all!" Sound familiar? But, after awhile, one sight blends into another and even the most amazing exhibit loses its appeal. A brief stop along the road to look and listen to a child's viewpoint can provide more learning than one might expect could be gained in such a short amount of time.

Figure 8.8.  Children long to touch what they see

Figure 8.9.  The pouncing tiger at the Smithsonian Natural
History Museum, Washington, D.C.

# 9

# Make a Collection or Two

Every day travelers visit new places and see new things. Children especially like to touch, feel, and handle new things. But much of what we see on vacation is kept behind glass windows. Museums, exhibits, and souvenir counters are all labeled "Don't Touch." Little fingers itch to touch in order to learn more. Help your childrens' explorations by adding to a collection already in progress, or begin one right on the spot on the basis of your kids' interests.

Some collections can be very expensive. The souvenir stands are filled with collector's items, which can add up as the miles go by. Moreover, most souvenirs reflect their common origin. It takes skill to sort among plastic Taiwanese items for a locally produced piece. Most children don't have this expertise and are attracted by colored chicken feathers on a rubber spear or a snow scene paperweight from Hong Kong.

"Can we buy something, Daddy? Can we?" The souvenir stand is just ahead. How can Daddy say no? After all, we *are* on vacation and it would be nice to stop and browse. Most fathers know that souvenir stand items will, in the next ten miles, probably cause some arguments or will break. What should Dad do?

He might begin by asking the kids to pause and reflect for a moment. Usually, the souvenir stand is conveniently located for browsing after viewing some attraction. Ask the children to think about what they have just seen and what memories they'd like to take with them. Ask them to choose their souvenirs accordingly. So many plastic toys, ceramic doodads, and Asian imports are then immediately eliminated from consideration. The object is not to buy a toy, but to look for something which will remind them of the things they saw and the fun they had, even when they are many miles away from here.

"Here's a little deer—just like the one we saw along the road this morning."

"Here's a cornhusk doll—just like the kind children used to play with years ago in the village we just saw."

"Here's a tepee decorated with the same design as the one we saw at the Indian festival."

These are specific examples of purchases which reinforce a learning experience. Even a "preoperational" three-year-old can, after seeing an elephant in the zoo, relate the experience to a small realistic model (not a fluffy stuffed pink elephant toy) that he can carry home with him. He may not be able to pronounce "elephant" very well, but the model will remind him of the real elephant for a longer time than he might otherwise remember. Certainly, as a child shows and tells others of his model or picture, the sharing experience itself becomes a reinforcing activity.

Among the least expensive souvenirs are postcards. For fifteen or twenty cents you can get professional pictures of the most familiar landmarks on your trip. It certainly saves film for your own family shots. But, especially for pint-size travelers, pictures are immediate reminders of something perhaps seen only minutes ago. When a child is faced with a rack of postcards, it's a test of his recall. Cries of "Oh, I saw that!" and "We've been there!" rekindle the excitement and interest of the scene captured on the postcard.

Other sources of picture souvenirs include the local chamber of commerce, always a good place to stop for information about events, directions, hours, and the community in general. Often, chamber of commerce brochures contain surprises—pictures of places you'd like to see but hadn't heard of before. And the brochures usually come filled with postcard-type photos of special spots. These are good cutting and pasting materials for scrapbooks.

Don't forget restaurant items. Eager to point out their locations, restaurant managers often display local maps and pictures on their menus, place mats, napkins, and paper coasters. If your child spills maple syrup or ketchup on his own, the waitress will usually be happy to supply you with an extra. It's good publicity for the restaurant and fine collection material for children.

Many other collections are free. Natural items, such as soil, rocks, shells, leaves, and feathers, make interesting collections for two reasons. First, as with other souvenirs, they remind you of the places you've been and the things you've seen and done. Second, natural items reflect regional environments. For ecological reasons there are often laws against picking wild flowers or hauling away rocks, particularly in national parks and forest preserves. These laws should be carefully followed. There's nothing worse than adding a large fine to the family's souvenir collection.

## COLLECTING SOIL

The most accessible and least controversial souvenir is plain earth, the soil, the basic ingredient of every environment. The red clay of Georgia, the black soil of the Midwest, the sands of the Southwest all tell their silent story of the types of vegetation and wildlife in those areas. Bear a few basic rules in mind when collecting soil samples. First, go beyond the highway, building, or parking lot area. Construction of those facilities inevitably meant a great deal of shifting land. In some cases, fill dirt was carried to the site from many miles away. Taking a sample from such a disturbed site probably would not represent the soil of the area. So be sure to move well beyond the shoulders of the highway or the area of construction. When you find an undisturbed spot, dig down an inch or more, beneath the layer of humus or decaying leaves. Take a small amount from the next layer.

A young child will notice different colors of soils gathered from different areas. Older children might compare such qualities as the depth of the topsoil layer, the texture of the soil (the size of the separate grains), and the structure of the soil (do the grains cling together?). A young teenager may relate different soil types with various kinds of crops he sees growing in separate areas. While climate is very influential in agricultural strategies, soil is the basic ingredient. Your child may not necessarily become a soil scientist but he will recognize that a handful of dirt is not as common as he had thought!

## COLLECTING ROCKS

Rocks are fun to collect. Since they're heavy, you might point out that small samples are just as attractive as large boulders. Remember that gravel is frequently transported for road and parking lot pavements, so when gathering samples from a region, move away from the disturbed area. Older collectors should label or number their rocks in order to identify the site where the rock was found.

The story of how rocks are formed is fascinating and is included in classroom materials at all levels. The differences between sedimentary, metamorphic, and igneous rocks are clearly illustrated and many children have been exposed to the terms. If your child doesn't know them, tuck a paperback rock manual into your suitcase.

Since rocks are the basic source of soil construction, their color tends to be similar to the ground where they lie. This is clearly seen if you place a rock from another region on the ground beside a newly found rock. Ask, "Which one belongs here? Why?"

## COLLECTING WATER SAMPLES

A Midwestern child's first taste of the ocean is an eye-opening experience. Have him take home some sea water to help remember its salty taste. Very little children sometimes believe that lake or river water gets dark at night. A bottleful collected at night and brought into the light can disprove that fallacy.

Comparing water taken at different places through a microscope is very rewarding for a young scientist (Figure 9.1). Your children might want to collect an exhibit of water from different places. Here are a few suggestions. Take samples from different levels of the same body of water. Contrast samples from a running stream and a stagnant pool. Collect samples from different locations along a river, particularly before and after that river flows through a large city or is joined

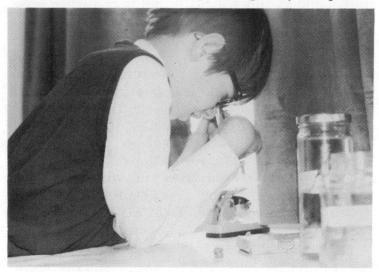

Figure 9.1. David compares water samples using a microscope

by a large tributary. The clear water of Lake Itasca, the Mississippi's source, contrasts spectacularly with the muddy current south of St. Louis.

Incidentally, some people have earned a considerable amount of money through vacation time water analyses. If you gather evidence of industrial pollution and the case stands in court, you receive monetary reward for your efforts! That takes well-documented proof, such as accurately labeled and dated samples and pictures. If you're interested in pursuing this type of investigation, contact the Environmental Protection Agency, 401 M Street, SW, Washington, D.C., for details. This type of problem is particularly appropriate for teenagers irritated by the world's injustices, but who can't see how to do anything about them!

Other natural items can be collected without damaging the environment if one is careful. Small pieces of driftwood and different types of bark can be found without stripping trees. Birds drop their feathers and empty eggshells. Butterflies succumb to the speed of passing autos.

The best place to find many natural items is in the overlooked space between the highway and the landowner's fence. Wild flowers often bloom in such profusion that one pressed blossom would not be missed. What may look barren to motorists often yields treasures to children released from the confines of the car for a few moments (Figure 9.2).

Superhighways stretch monotonously for miles. Ask, "See if you can find something about this spot that makes it different from the others." What a challenge! If the young researchers already have a collection or two in mind, these can give them guidance and direction. You may wish

Figure 9.2.   Children search for treasure alongside the road

to take some preparatory measures before leaving home. Stock up on paperback manuals and field guides to help get the most from your family's observations. The Golden Nature Guide series are clear and simplified guides.[1]

The nature of any collection takes on greater significance if it is organized into a meaningful whole. It's tempting to say, "I'll get the sample now and label it later" or "Let's put it all together when we get home." Remember that the here-and-now is most important for a child; that is where and when curiosity is aroused. The satisfaction of seeing a meaningful collection grow does a great deal to encourage curiosity to arise again, another day and another place. This is so much better than saying, "We'll do it later, Son."

[1]Published by Golden Press, New York.

## SUPPLIES

Your collector will need containers, though not many and not too large. Restricting the size may help your children be more selective in their search for small items. EGG CARTONS are perfect for saving small rocks or eggshells. An old TELEPHONE DIRECTORY or MAIL-ORDER CATALOGUE is excellent for pressing leaves or flowers. CIGAR BOXES hold small pieces of driftwood or feathers. Although BABY FOOD JARS are best for soil samples, they may be bulky to carry. SMALL PLASTIC BAGS travel better.

## MAKE A TRIP BOOK

For younger children, a review of the collected items of the day is especially important. A trip book which organizes daily paper or picture finds on a two-page spread can be a source of delight that evening and years later (see Figure 9.3). Remember to bring a SCRAPBOOK, GLUE, SCISSORS, and some CRAYONS. Pasting down a memory holds it in the mind a bit longer. Preschoolers could dictate a descriptive line or two for you to add to the page. Now, don't cheat—years later their dictated words will be much more interesting than your interpretation of what you think should have been said!

Some items simply can't be brought home and substitutions have to be made. If you're venturing into wilderness, a small amount of PLASTER-OF-PARIS stowed in the luggage will record interesting wildlife tracks to take home. Mix the plaster with a little water and pour it into an animal's footprint.

Figure 9.3.   Making a trip book

Figure 9.4.   "Capturing" a bird's nest in the sand

The mixture will soon harden in the form of the track.

Film is another method to "capture" wildlife in natural settings. A bird's nest found in the sand is best left undisturbed, but a picture series of nests of all kinds makes a delightful and less cumbersome collection (Figure 9.4). Film is also useful for remembering a still-life scene. The shells in Figure 9.5 were not found in that position; the beauty of each one enhanced the others when placed together. The whole family created the grouping—each adding a favorite piece—and the end result was a picture of a family collection.

The act of collecting itself is usually more rewarding than the end result. The excitement of the find, sharing it with others, and comparing it with previous finds makes collecting such an interesting activity.

Figure 9.5.   Create a still life for the family collection

One final word of caution. It's usually not wise to contrast collections across age levels. While five-year-old Mary is interested in seeing the wiggly things through her brother's microscope, she also needs to feel pride and a sense of achievement in her own collection of rocks. When each takes pleasure in watching the others' growing collections, everyone will benefit from a meaningful, shared activity that will extend far beyond the collections themselves.

# 10

# Snap a Picture

Almost every family lugs a camera along on their trips. But cameras frequently become a source of family contention the minute the family is on the road. "If David can take pictures with his own camera, why can't I?" complains John. (The four years' age difference is ignored in that remark.) "Me, too!" Mary chimes in, and she's two years younger than John. David, camera in hand, immediately begins snapping so that by the first rest stop he has gone through an entire roll of film.

"Change my film for me? Please?"

"What could you have taken pictures of while we were driving!"

"Well, there was this cat on a barn roof. And then I saw a white horse and Dad said to watch for white horses so I took his picture but he was running. And there were some birds sitting on the phone wires, and I don't remember what the other pictures are."

Later, we learn that the rest of the film features Mary's right eyeball, the back of John's head, and seven black frames because David turned the film too fast. There must be a better way! But do adults use cameras any more successfully? A review of typical tourist pictures features "Mom and Dad in front of Mt. Rushmore," "Children in front of the Statue of Liberty," and "Aunt Bessie on the Capitol steps."

Magazines are making us more aware of creative photo work. Is it necessary to take pictures of local scenery or national monuments if a postcard collection could do the job for us just as well? Certainly, postcard pictures would be of better quality. Most people only pick up a camera during the two weeks they are on vacation, and the manipulation of its various levers and openings is often more of a puzzle than an aid to good photography. So why take a camera at all? Often, things happen on a trip that are fun to capture and add to later family memories. The expression on your child's face as he sees his first redwood tree is probably of more value to you than the tree itself. And you will never find *that* on a postcard!

Action shots are always more exciting than those where family members line up like a rogues' gallery, facing the camera with wooden smiles. Mary is so intent on keeping the treadle of the spinning wheel going that the intrusion of the camera is hardly noticed. Certainly a picture like that helps a child remember better after you have returned home.

A simple camera can be used to show action. A

young child may have trouble taking action shots but that's not necessary to show movement. Some things, such as a giraffe eating lunch, happen slowly enough to make action photography much simpler. The sequence of an event or the steps of a process, snapped separately, tell a story when developed. The pictures in Figures 10.1 and 10.2 are not very effective seen alone. But together they can show contrasts, such as differences in water levels as a ship lies in locks at the Sault Sainte Marie Canals between Canada and Michigan.

Try to capture the spirit of the moment in family shots. Don't wait for your child to stare directly at you, with a clean face beneath neatly combed hair. After all, did you spend your vacation taking showers every ten minutes? Or did you have fun doing things? Some children actively object to having their pictures taken and frequently the

Figure 10.1. The water is at its lowest level in this picture of the locks of the Sault Sainte Marie Canal

Figure 10.2. The water at its highest level in the Sault Sainte Marie Canal locks

cause can be traced to all of those nagging requests made before the shutter is clicked. "Smile this way. Stand up straighter. Don't you ever comb your hair?" Pictures should be fun to take, otherwise the memories they recall will be just as unpleasant as the original scene.

Not every shot needs to be filled with family members. Mary made special friends with a ranger who helped her overcome her fear of the donkeys. Shouldn't we take his picture? John's special request for apple pie à la mode plus whipped cream was filled by a waitress along Route I-90. Shouldn't we take a picture of her special smile as she served the pie? Remembering special people met even briefly brings back lovely, warm memories long after the trip is over.

People needn't always be the central subject of a picture. There are many other good subjects.

Hurricanes along the Atlantic bring tremendous amounts of driftwood and shells to the beaches, but we can't carry them all home. The shells are too numerous to count and the driftwood is too heavy. The solution is in the camera. Interesting shots from a variety of angles can capture the uniqueness of the driftwood and its beauty in its natural setting. The same can be true of the rocks of the Grand Canyon or the sand of the Painted Desert. Try different angles and close shots. Point the camera right down into the center of a group of wild flowers and snap. You will then be able to take them home even though you have been kind enough to leave them growing for others to enjoy. Such subjects make interesting collections.

The child able to work a camera can limit excessive shutter clicking if he concentrates on finding unique and appropriate examples. Birds and animals are nice to snap, but they are often too elusive for young photographers. When the subject is caged, the photo will usually feature more bars than animal. Children have more success if they aim at something large and immobile like a building.

Pictures of objects which are collected into a series are quite educational, both while the young researcher focuses his camera, and later when he lays out the results side by side. If the trip is to be lengthy, you could use distinctive examples of local architecture to emphasize different building materials available in various parts of the country. Homes in different geographical areas make interesting contrasts. The wooden frame houses of New Jersey contrast dramatically with Southwestern adobe buildings. One of the oldest

European-style homes in the United States, in St. Augustine, Florida, predates by several centuries the log cabins in a restored Midwestern pioneer village. Again, both examples illustrate the use of local materials and the level of technological ability available during the time of construction.

Whether or not these "vernacular" constructions are really architecture is questionable to many authorities on architecture. Well, what *is* architecture? Most authorities state that, in order to be an architectural example, a building must meet three criteria. It must be functional; i.e., it should serve the purpose for which it was designed. It must also have form, some type of artistic quality that expresses beauty. Finally, it must have permanence or an enduring quality. Each of these criteria can be a source of philosophical questions when you and your family are faced with "a piece of architecture." For example, does a building's form control its function, or does the function of a building decide what form its design must take? Your children may be very involved in this question without even realizing it. "Open classroom" and "team teaching" educational methods have resulted in school buildings designed with few inner walls because many teachers find traditional school architecture restrictive. Here lies the question of priority. Should the form of a building control its function or vice versa?

Other examples of this issue can be found in buildings you'll see on your trip. The U.S. Capitol is the most famous example. George Washington approved the original plan and pointed out its "grandeur, simplicity and convenience." For almost two centuries, the Capitol has housed the legislative and, for a time, the judicial branch of the federal government in rooms continually outgrown and redesigned. The bicameral structure of the legislature influenced the choice of architectural form: equally balanced wings on either side of the Capitol. The abandoned, outgrown rooms caused Congress to search for better uses for them, and the old form took on a new function, such as Statuary Hall. Form and function certainly have an effect upon each other.

Another philosophical issue your family might consider is the expression of beauty in various structures you view. Someone, sometime, probably thought that "awful" design before you was beautiful. Probably, different members of your family will express their own views of what is beautiful. Take this concrete opportunity to move into an abstract idea. There is the building; it's an object we can all see. To the architect it represents beauty. But, because each of us have different values and different viewpoints, we may disagree with the architect's idea of beauty. The most difficult problem with this topic is that it frequently draws monosyllabic answers from children.

"Do you like that building?"

"Yeah, I guess so."

"Why?"

"Oh, it's kinda pretty."

That takes us nowhere fast! We'll need to ask about specific details of the building and perhaps introduce some contrasts.

"What do you think is the prettiest part of the

building? Look at the windows and the decoration above them. Do you like that part? Is this building more attractive to you than the one we saw yesterday? Why?"

When contrasting architecture, whether by period or source of influence, look closely at the doorways and the windows of various structures. These are both areas of utility and creative expression. The tops or capitals of pillars have three basic styles—Doric, Ionic, and Corinthian—and their variations, and it's possible to stand in one spot on Pennsylvania Avenue in Washington, D.C., and see all three. Children who previously consulted encyclopedia drawings could be all prepared with their sketches for comparison with the real examples (Figure 10.3). Focusing on different aspects of architecture helps children determine those things which make a difference to them, the difference between their ideas of "pretty" and "plain."

"I like that building because it's big."

Ask, "Is it big and beautiful or big and ugly? Because it is big, does that make it important?"

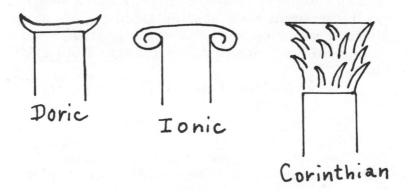

Figure 10.3. Styles of pillar architecture

Exploring questions of value can clarify your child's thinking about his own preferences. There are many adults who can't clearly explain what or why they like something. Early experience with expressed feelings and supportive reasoning helps children avoid this confusion as they grow up.

"I guess I like the steeple on the top best," David decides.

This is where the camera comes into action. David focuses in on the part of the building he likes best because the steeple says something of value to him (Figure 10.4). He may decide to continue snapping steeples as he finds them. Later comparisons will show him architectural differences he may not have noticed at first glance.

Church architecture is a study in itself and the

Figure 10.4.   Steeple of a building

contrasts are unlimited. One trip yielded the group of photos in figures 10.5–10.7. Each church was snapped for an entirely different reason. The large stone church on the hill was built in Maryland in 1798, but its historical value predates that period by more than a century. Established in 1662 by Father Andrew White, it is the oldest continuously run parish in the United States. The dark brown wooden church stands in Iowa and is part of the tradition of millions of Americans who have sung "The Little Brown Church in the Vale." The little

Figure 10.5.   Stone church built in 1798

Figure 10.6. "The Little Brown Church in the Vale"

white church on a country road in West Virginia is uniquely octagonal in form.

Other public buildings such as state capitols, county courthouses, and restaurants make interesting comparisons. Compare libraries throughout the Midwest if you're searching for similarities. Andrew Carnegie funded the building of two basic library plans which appear repeatedly in small towns in Iowa.

Occasionally, you might find old-fashioned architecture used to create fantasy moods. Amusement parks and some shopping centers re-create

Figure 10.7.  Octagonal church in West Virginia

the Old West through storefront façades and
wooden sidewalks. Ask "What feeling do these
buildings give you? Why do you think they're designed like this?" Compare snapshots of such
places with history book illustrations. Older children might compare pictures of the copy with
those of the original to search for anachronisms—
some feature on the model which is inappropriate
to the style and period of the original.

Try some thematic approaches while taking
pictures. During one family trip, David, John, and
Mary looked for pictures illustrating the theme of
energy. They found subjects everywhere and they
soon learned to discriminate between sources and
uses of energy. After the pictures were developed,
they were sorted according to the sequence of

energy production and consumption. The hydroelectric generators at Niagara Falls and the huge coal-digging machine in western Ohio were labeled "sources." The power lines were labeled "carriers," the power company, a "distributor," and the auto factory, a "user." The pictures placed in sequence (Figures 10.8 through 10.12) told a story about energy that the children could find in almost any encyclopedia. The essential difference was the level of their involvement, both in gathering and analyzing data.

What about the younger children in the family? If they can't manipulate a camera successfully, need they be left out of the activities? Not necessarily. Younger children may have different interests than the rest of the family, but if the trip is to be memorable for everyone, their memories should be on film too. Young children can also be excellent directors of others' photography.

"Mary, look around you. What three pictures should I take for you so that you can remember this place when we get home?" Even though Mary won't snap the shutter herself, her attention is focused on what is most valuable to her. Limiting her encourages a thorough examination in order to select her three choices. In fact, such limitations would be good for older children as well.

When a child becomes a camera enthusiast, one important rule to remember is that pictures taken from a speeding car are rarely of much value when developed. If the picture is worth taking, then it's worth a stop. As a vehicle of learning, organizing, and remembering patterns, photography contributes much more to the trip than simply photo album material.

Figure 10.8. Hydroelectric generators at Niagara Falls

Figure 10.9. Coal-digging machine in western Ohio

# CARRIERS

Figure 10.10.   Power lines

# DISTRIBUTOR

Figure 10.11.   Power company plant

Figure 10.12.   Automobile factory

# 11

# Make the Most of the Media

Travelers are isolated people. Their cars move down the highway like small space capsules, isolating them from close contact with the environment around them. Brief contact with others—a gas station attendant, waitress, desk clerk—is often only perfunctory. A traveler just passing through rarely pauses to reflect on the way of life in different towns which service his car and shelter his family. An overnight stop often isn't long enough to gain more than superficial knowledge of a place and its people.

Isolated from home routines, travelers frequently lose contact with the rest of the world too. Events occur so rapidly, a Middle East war could begin and end unbeknownst to a sightseeing tourist. Some people seek this kind of isolation in order to find complete relaxation. But most people like to know what's happening in their world.

Some people stop early enough during the day so they can watch the evening news on the motel TV set. If you follow that routine, be sure to check the local news in addition to national and international news. Local items can give you a closer glimpse of your new environment.

The medium of television is probably very familiar to your children. It can be a useful tool to demonstrate to all ages similarities and differences between this new place and home. The youngest child spies the TV set and, remembering it's cartoon time at home, is surprised if something different appears on the screen. Take this opportunity to clarify the concept of distance. Ask, "Remember how long we drove today? Every minute we were in the car took us further from home. Watch the TV and see if you can find anything that's like what you see at home."

Typically, children react to scheduling differences negatively, complaining, "The dumb people here really messed things up!" Again, here's an opportunity to ask if things which are different are really "dumb" or "messed up." Show how another point of view isn't necessarily wrong. Older children can listen to the local news to see just how "local" it is. A felt-tip marker and an extra map of the area laid out on the motel room desk are all the necessary materials. Have the child place an X over the city where the station originates, and another over the town where he is located. Each time the newscaster mentions a town where an event occurred, the child can locate it and draw a circle around it. He or she can analyze the result to see if the TV coverage area is large or small, and whether the town where he is spending the night is on the fringe of the service area or is centrally located. Teenagers can analyze the content of local news programming to determine the kinds of news deemed most important to that area's viewers. How different is it from your home area?

Newspapers from different towns along your route can provide raw material for similar analyses. There are a couple of advantages in using newspapers rather than television. First of all, newspapers are concrete objects and can be handled in a variety of ways. Second, printed news is not limited to a certain time slot in the day's activities. But, children are generally less familiar with newspapers, which may or may not be an advantage for your particular child. Unfamiliar things can be thought of as strange, interesting, or overwhelming, depending on your child's age and attitudes.

Small town newspapers reflect local news. If you are planning to spend some time in an area, be sure to pick up the paper for news of local events, celebrations, and exhibits which might prove interesting to your family.

As you travel from one town to the next, you'll note obvious differences in their size. A less obvious difference lies in their function as centers of economic activity. Geographers have classified different communities and their approximate populations as follows: hamlet (100), village (500), town (1,500), small city or county seat (6,000), regional city (60,000), regional metropolis (250,000), and national metropolis (over one million).[1] These differently sized communities per-

---

1. Brian J. L. Berry, *Geography of Market Centers and Retail Distribution* (Englewood N. J.: Prentice-Hall), 1967), p. 21.

form a hierarchy of economic functions for their populations. A hamlet may have only one or two businesses and perhaps a gas station at the crossroads with a snack shop or a small grocery inside. But the hamlet residents would have to go to a town in order to obtain the services of a dentist, a bank, or a hardware store. Towns frequently have newspapers published on a weekly basis. The next level, a small city or county seat, may or may not have a daily or semiweekly paper. A daily newspaper usually requires the population level of a regional city in order to be profitable. Since each of the higher level functions of a hierarchy serve both that level and the smaller levels beneath it, you'll find regional city newspapers delivered to small towns and hamlets many miles away. The *New York Times*, a publication of a national metropolis, can be found at newsstands all over the country.

The boundaries of newspapers' service areas can be estimated by noting what is available for sale at a newsstand. If you stay in a community over a weekend, you may find different papers available on a weekday as opposed to a Sunday. Some consideration should be given to the number of tourists that the newsstand serves. If that community has a large tourist trade, they may supply newspapers which would not ordinarily be in demand by local residents. An older child could analyze the contents of a newsstand in the same manner used to analyze the territory included in local television news. In fact, a comparison between the reach of the television station and the newspapers provides further information for judging where the community fits in the hierarchy of functions.

Still another source of information is the yellow pages of the phone book located in your motel room. Have the child choose three different products and/or services, such as physicians, bicycles, and clothing stores listed in the yellow pages. Then all they need to do is count how many businesses supply each of the three products or services. A chart of several towns listing the number of businesses in the three categories provides data for comparative analyses. Population figures would also contribute to a better understanding.

To adults, the facts are obvious—you have to go to a big city to obtain a unique product or service. But, it's quite an intellectual achievement for a child to analyze the reasons why. The result is a comment like, "Oh, so that's why only some towns have grain elevators" or "Now I know why there are so many office buildings in the city."

Newspapers also provide inexpensive clipping material for children's scrapbooks (see Chapter 10). Activities for younger children include:

- Clipping the name of the town and the dateline from the front page, pasting them to a sheet of paper, and drawing a picture of the most interesting things in the town.
- Clipping the weather report and comparing it with the day's weather.
- Clipping pictures from ads for local products.
- Cutting out headlines which correspond with postcard pictures of town sights.
- Clipping pictures that reflect the season of the year.
- Cutting out pictures of sports activities that reflect the local interests of the region.

Younger children love to clip and paste or

color, and news photos are often more educational than traditional coloring books. A collection of photos that appear in several newspapers can help children recognize prominent citizens.

Older children may enjoy:

- Examining the front page to determine important news on the local, state, and federal levels.
- Examining the classified section to see the kinds of jobs, services, and products that are available in that community.
- Reading editorials and letters to the editor to find out the important issues of the day, according to the members of a particular community.
- Examining the sports page for local interest in recreational activities.

These activities increase in educational value when two or more papers are compared. If your trip is a cross-country "quickie," you might pick up local papers at rest stops or lunch stops. Keep in mind that the papers will fill the back seat unless you confine the collection to specific sections: front pages, editorial pages, or merely headlines and datelines, depending on the ages and interests of your children. Political cartoons appearing in papers reflect attitudes toward major issues. Sometimes these political cartoons are syndicated and appear in many papers; other times they are local in origin. Within a two or three day period, you may run across the same cartoon or editorial in several different papers. A teenager would be able to compare the attitudes of several papers toward that one issue. Ask, "Is the viewpoint expressed by the cartoon supported by all of these local papers?"

Media—newspapers, television, telephone

books—provide a closer view of the people's lives in the areas you visit. Of course, the same kind of study can be made on your home community, but comparisons and contrasts are enhanced by collecting data from a greater number of samples. And the best part about media studies is that curiosity about new places is aroused in advance. If enthusiasm is also maintained, your child will want to find out as much as possible through all the forms of media.

# 12

# Look for Hidden Meanings

"Who's that man in the park?"

"What man?"

"That big man—that statue."

"Well, let's see. The best way to find out is to read the inscription on the base of the statue."

But sometimes the inscription is illegible, meaningless, or missing. Then identifying the statue can become a mystery adventure. Looking beneath the pigeons at the bases of statues and monuments can be very enlightening. Try asking local people about the statue. (That can be quite an experience in itself.) Usually smaller and older communities have many residents who know all about the few statues and monuments located in their area. That's not usually true of city dwellers. In most cities, there are so many statues by the buildings and in the parks, people aren't always sure of who they represent or why they've been erected.

Sometimes, searching for clues about the statue is more interesting than the statue itself. If it's a prominent landmark, then naturally it will be recorded on postcards and the chamber of commerce will have a pile of relevant information. It's the obscure monuments that can lead you down interesting paths. Local museums, historical societies or city government offices may have some suggestions. Overall, the final identification of stone men on horses is far less important than the process of discovery. Responses to questions can be very revealing of local attitudes toward the establishment, maintenance, and preservation of statues or monuments.

A statue reflects the values of the people who commissioned its erection. The care of the statue, its landscaped setting, and its prominence in local tourist information indicate the feeling of kinship between the people who live now and the event or person represented by the statue. Some structures never seem to lose their popular appeal. The Lincoln Memorial, the Statue of Liberty, and Mount Rushmore exemplify monuments that have stood the test of time. Other monuments that once held great meaning have been allowed to deteriorate unnoticed. The ideals that they once represented are lost until one asks, "Who is that on the horse?"

Monuments are also interesting because they reflect the style and sentiment of the period in which they were commissioned, as well as the event which they represent. Sometimes the materials used are local; other times they have been imported from great distances. The story behind the Washington Monument is well documented. The arguments, architectural changes, and the frustrations in financing construction are conveyed by pictures and mementos exhibited in the base. Even young children will notice different colors of stone on the outside of the monument. These indicate places where construction was halted for a period of years. Even if you don't wish to walk up or down the many flights of steps inside the monument, you could step inside the stairwell for a brief glimpse of the stone sent from the quarries of many states and nations. The contrasts are interesting examples of geological variations, as well as visual symbols of the states and nations that helped in the construction of the monument.

The monument at Plymouth Rock in Massachusetts exemplifies a very different style of commemoration. The barrenness of Plymouth Rock has been draped with a pillared stone shelter and on the nearby hill, the monument to the Pilgrims (erected in the nineteenth century) is encircled by figures symbolic of education, justice, and morality. At the time of its construction, people may have felt very differently toward the monument than do we. Monuments and statues are intended to arouse feelings in those who view them. Yet, the passage of time may foster some totally unintended reactions. Plymouth Rock was seen as a symbol of outrage by a group of Indians who staged a Thanksgiving demonstration there just a few years ago.

Symbolism is a difficult concept for children to understand, but statues are concrete objects. As such, they are useful in explaining abstract ideas.

The Statue of Liberty is a concrete symbol of the abstract idea of freedom. The poem by Emma Lazarus, inscribed at the base of the statue, translates the symbolism into literary description for older children. But younger children can look at pictures of arriving immigrants and understand the feelings their faces express at their first sight of America. Ask, "Why did all those people come to America? What did they want? What kinds of feelings did they have when they saw the land after so many days at sea? What did the statue mean to them? Does the statue just signify a woman in a robe, or does it also convey a special feeling that's more important?"

Ideas don't flow freely from some children. Their responses must be guided.

"Johnny, you live in America and you know what America is supposed to be about. What do you think the statue on top of this nation's capitol building is all about?"

"Well, she's holding a book, sort of like the Statue of Liberty."

"What do you think the book is about?"

"I don't know."

"What do people have in a country that can be written in a book?"

"Laws, I guess."

"Does the statue look happy or sad, hopeful or mad? What kinds of feelings do you think she has?"

"She looks like she's looking a long way off."

"Maybe she is; maybe she's looking into the future."

Musing like this enhances children's awareness of some of the expressions of symbolism. This is not only useful in understanding the meaning of statues; it is also an essential skill for dealing meaningfully with the ceremony, literature, propaganda, and drama encountered in daily life.

How important are these monuments and their symbolism in the lives of the people? How do people think about symbols of law and freedom? Is it important that these values be expressed? What do people value? In recent years, educators have been concerned with the issue of values education and the controversial question, "Should values be taught in the classroom?" Actually, values *are* taught, not only in the classroom, but everywhere. They are taught by example, accepted without question, or rejected without investigation. The result is confusion and conflict. Therefore, focus on the clarification rather than the teaching of values. Help your children to investigate, identify, and seek the justifications behind values expressed in peoples' actions.

Our example here is monuments which were dedicated by a group of people in another time, in order to immortalize a value held dear to them. It can be an enriching family experience to take a few minutes to consider if you and your children share that same value or if modern times have rendered the old ideal obsolete.

You can clarify values by identifying criteria which determine whether something is of value to someone. For example, a value is freely chosen from alternatives after careful consideration of the consequences. A value is prized, publicly affirmed, and acted upon repeatedly.[1] A monument or statue

---

[1] Louis Raths, Merrill Harmin, and Sidney Simon, *Values and Teaching* (Columbus, Ohio: Charles E. Merrill, 1966).

is not, by itself, a value. But someone placed a value on a deed or an ideal and eventually a commemorative monument was raised. It's impossible to thoroughly analyze the motives and depths of the values held by people in the past. But guesses can be made which can be compared with family values.

A statue on a courthouse lawn in honor of the Civil War dead from Allamakee County in Iowa (Figure 12.1) raised questions. "What kinds of values might have been involved in the decision to erect the statue? What do you think was important to those people then?"

Mary thought a bit and then said, "Maybe people felt sorry about their friends dying."

"Maybe," said David, "they were proud they had helped fight for our country."

Figure 12.1. Statue on a courthouse lawn

"Maybe the people who stayed home wanted to do something about the war, too," added John.

Where in all this are the stated or implied values? Consider this statement: We value the memory of people who died for their country. Sounds good, doesn't it? Noble, anyway. And the sentiment undoubtedly was part of the values of those who contributed to raising the memorial. Now the thing to do is to determine if we would support statements which embody values of the past. "Can anyone remember something that would prove *we* value the memory of people who died for their country?"

"I remember studying about Nathan Hale in school and he was a good guy."

"We fly our flag on Memorial Day."

"I remember when the guy down the street got killed in Viet Nam and Mom took a casserole to his folks."

"But why did those guys have to get killed? Why didn't they just mind their own business and not fight?"

Therein lies the basis for a discussion which might absorb the family for the rest of the trip! This is also an example of one advantage of a family trip as compared with a school outing. The opinions of class members are very important when a youngster is involved with his peer group. But the opinions of different age groups are important too. While a teacher may be involved in such discussions, his or her major responsibility is to clarify values held by different people. A teacher may also help students decide what their own values are; that is, to clarify those values they already hold. Parents, on the other hand, may discuss beliefs and values with family members on the basis of what they feel is morally correct.

Bicentennial interest encouraged many communities to catalogue the monuments and statues in their public areas. Books describing and detailing the histories of these structures are generally available. All the statues and monuments in Washington, D.C., have recently been catalogued. Washington, the center of America's historical and political life, has become the focal point of many efforts to commemorate deeds and their heroes, events and their heroines.

Similar cataloguing efforts have reached far beyond Capitol Hill. Many people in search of their roots traipse through their local cemeteries checking headstones and mapping locations. Visiting cemeteries can be a unique experience for children, especially if you're tracing a family tree. But even if you're not, the inscriptions on older headstones make fascinating reading (Figure 12.2).

Some monuments are not made of sculptured stone, but are memorials nevertheless. The mapped history of America often looks like a web of lines across the continent. Americans have always been on the go and many of the trails opened by Indians, explorers, trappers, and settlers are now highways across the nation. Some of the more famous ones are marked: the Mohawk Trail, the Lewis and Clark Trail, the Oregon Trail, and the Natchez Trace. Children enjoy looking for things along the route which have changed since the original trail was blazed. You could also compare and contrast the purposes of the original travelers with your own.

Figure 12.2.   David reads a headstone inscription

Occasionally, you'll find a monument that's just plain laughable. Like marking the spot where the largest pancake was cooked or the biggest sundae created! A man in Iowa got so tired of all the roadside markers and commemorations during Bicentennial celebrations that he erected a sign on his lawn stating that "Two hundred years ago nothing happened here." But even comical monuments say something about what's important to people. A monumental occasion is many things to many people and a peek under the pigeons may give you a closer look at other people's values.

# 13

# Visit with the People

A young couple watched the glass blower at work in Jamestown, Virginia. The girl was absorbed in the technique used to fashion the handle on a pitcher. She read the descriptive signs and the folder and carefully observed the process. She learned quite a bit about glassblowing in colonial times.

Suddenly, she looked around and realized she was alone in the crowd of tourists. After wandering about the small building, she finally found her husband deep in conversation with a small group of glass blowers on their break. He, too, was learning about glassblowing in colonial times *and* about working conditions in a tourist center.

We learn to stand by passively during process demonstrations because we do the same thing at home in front of the television set. But a trip gives us the advantage of being able to visit with the people. Most people enjoy talking about what they do for a living and about their lives. The secret to encouraging such conversations is just to listen and show interest. You can learn so much that way.

Children often need to improve their listening skills. Kids tend to interrupt with enthusiastic comments or wander off in the middle of an explanation. To help develop your child's attention span, encourage him to listen to something carefully so he can explain it later to his friends at home. Acquiring information for later retelling makes a person listen much more closely to the original explanation.

It's fun to watch and listen to people in action. The tour group itself can be a good study in sociology! Remember the sociologist's question, "How do people behave in groups?" People's reactions to each other, to you, to your family, and to the guide can be a fascinating study. Some of the people you will see are in familiar groups; others are reacting to strangers in a strange situation.

If your family is camping, the kids will meet lots of other people of all ages. Children are generally less inhibited than adults and will talk to anyone about anything as they wander about the campground or swing at the playground.

"We live in Maryland. That's a long way," announces Mary.

"We live in Michigan. That's a longer way," says the little boy on the next swing.

"We have a big blue tent," Mary continues.

"Ours is green and has two rooms."

"We have a camper on wheels," a third child chimes in.

The kids are playing a verbal game called, "Can you top this?" The game is not limited to children; people of all ages engage in it. The rules are as follows: (1) make a statement that "tops" the last fellow's claim, and (2) don't really listen or express interest in the other guy's statement except to search for a way to "top" it. With a little parental guidance, older children can identify these rules in action as they listen to Mary's conversation, or by listening to people anywhere—at the gas station or in line at an amusement park. Why bother to learn about these interaction games people play? Certainly not for the purpose of pointing out "bad" behavior on the part of other people; rather, children's observations will guide them in future personal interactions.

We mentioned standing in line. That's wearisome, but if you visit any popular spot at peak season, it's inevitable that your family will spend time in line. However, it's a great opportunity for quietly observing other people's behavior.

Nonverbal communication is a field all by itself. People standing in line are variously patient, eager, tired, frustrated, or bored. Watch for those expressions on their faces and in their posture. While these feelings are usually kept within and not communicated verbally to strangers, watch closely. Somehow, a feeling is communicated. The line begins to move forward; people smile and appear to relax or they might surge forward with determination. The mood of a group may vary with the temperature, the time of day, and the length of the wait. A child whines and fusses. How do the people near him react? Is there a smile of sympathy from the hot, tired mother or a frown of irritation? Of course, it's impossible to stand in line with children and comfortably discuss these little dramas around you. Introduce the kids to the concept in private.

A beach or a picnic area is ideal for observation. There, families park themselves and their equipment for whole afternoons of sun and fun. Groups and individuals "stake out" pieces of territory at the beach or picnic ground, and their nonverbal message is quite clear. They seem to be announcing "This is *our* area," as they spread their towels and set up their folding chairs. Ask your child, "How do you know that spot on the beach is being used? Watch for a while and see what happens as other people approach or set up their chairs nearby." The action may be especially interesting if the beach is crowded. People, with a lot of space at their disposal, usually appear less concerned at the loss of some nearby territory.

Nonverbal behavior can be observed in restaurants, on public transportation, on elevators, or at doorways. To reinforce something they may already have observed, ask the children to act out a small scene without speaking. For example, have them try the typical scene of indecision at a doorway. The words aren't spoken, but everyone gets the message:

"You go first."

"No, after you."

"Well, all right."

"Whoops—are you going, or aren't you?"

Understanding nonverbal behavior helps children clarify situations in their own lives. It also helps them to be more or less expressive in their own nonverbal interactions with people as they judge impact.

A small town café is an excellent setting for investigating social behavior. Stop for morning coffee or an afternoon soda break and watch the action. Probably there will be small groups all around you. Does the waitress know everyone? What is the level of familiarity within the separate groups and between the groups? Are first names or last names used? Does anyone appear to stand out as a leader?

It's usually impossible to determine the complete situation in so brief a time. The most vocal person in a group frequently holds less group respect than a quiet man sitting in the background. The power structure in a group of quiet conversationalists is difficult to judge. During heated exchanges, it's sometimes possible to determine who has the final say or who makes the final decision. But it's rare to find such scenes in small towns where everyone usually knows everyone else. That kind of display is more typical among tired travelers who may argue openly, safe in anonymity.

Visits to informal places like small cafés needn't be the only times for quiet observation. Engage someone in conversation. Ask about a local landmark or industry or just chat about the weather. Now you are like the anthropologist or sociologist, a participant observer.

Small talk dealing primarily with the weather occupies almost everyone. Children can listen for it and judge its utility. Why discuss the weather sixteen times a day? Is it the weather that really matters or is it simply a way to ease initial strain between strangers? Compare the manners of different waiters and waitresses you encounter during your trip. What, if anything, do they say to your family? Children can discuss how different opening remarks cause them to feel differently about the person. The value of that piece of knowledge in later life is obvious!

One of the best sources of information in our society is frequently overlooked. Older folks are receptacles of fascinating memories that can breathe life into the past. Many older people retire to warmer climates and so are often found in vacation areas with much time and many memories to share. Children conversing with an older person can learn so much more about the flavor of the past than a book can ever tell them.

A final suggestion for observing social behavior involves signs—those constant, negative reminders that line the walls and highways of our lives. The sign in the laundromat, "Do not dye in this machine," and the one in the motel, "No noise after 10:00 P.M.," are restrictive for protective reasons. Ask your child to list the no-no signs he finds and then to consider their purposes. Occasionally he may find one he thinks is unfair, whose justification may take a bit of investigation. He might also wonder why people need all these rules and if these rules are followed all the time.

Some of the questions raised in this chapter might lead to some original social research on the part of an older child or a teenager. He or she could ask brief questions, relating to some current issue, of other people encountered during several weeks of travel. Then, tabulated responses could provide enough evidence to support or reject a hypothesis about people's feelings, opinions, or attitudes. Some books listed in the bibliography may be of value to you and your child in guiding the research.

One final word. Don't isolate conversation and observation from other ideas presented earlier. Talking with people is a basic communication skill that improves with analysis and practice. Well-traveled children know that the shortest way to find answers is to ask a question of a guide or the nearest knowledgeable person. Their quest for information lifts them beyond self-conscious shyness. Their success builds confidence in their ability to understand and deal with the world. Encourage talking, but also help your child to listen.

# 14

# Remembering

A trip lives on in memory long after the suitcases have been unpacked and the giant loads of laundry filtered of sand. If one of your goals was to build good memories of shared time together, then concrete reminders will be essential. Memory retention is very short for most of us and young children easily become confused and forgetful. Five-year-old Mary doesn't remember her infancy but she giggles through family movies and loves to reminisce, "Remember the time you took me to the ocean and I crawled in the sand?" It's only a movie of herself at sixteen months that she remembers, but what difference does it make? She still shares in a family memory which might otherwise have been lost to her.

Pictures and paper souvenirs pasted in a scrapbook, time lines, and collections all serve the same purpose. Each good time is relived again.

Surprisingly, the arguments over when and where to stop for lunch are forgotten and the flat tire fiasco becomes an amusing story about a temporarily frustrating experience. Playing "I remember when . . ." can remind a family of the warmth of summer all through the cold winter to follow.

But, beyond sentiment, trip memories can be very useful to children. In September, they're bound to be faced with the traditional question, "What did you do on your summer vacation?" Any of the projects or investigations mentioned in earlier chapters can be summarized and shared with the class in a variety of ways: as an oral report, a bulletin board, or a collection display. With parental help, children can prepare slide shows of trip highlights to share with their classmates. It doesn't matter if there are only one or two slides. The act of telling what they know about a distant place is what is important. They've been there and maybe no one else in the class has. That makes them an authority and helps raise self-confidence.

A strategy which helps sort out memories by time and place is useful for organizing both school reports and family memories. Spread a map out on the floor. Make sure it covers the area of your travels. Then arrange your pictures and souvenirs according to where they were obtained. If it's impossible to pile all that stuff on a map it can be stacked near the edge. With some string or yarn, encircle the piles and fasten the ends on the place where the things were gathered. For example, suppose the family toured the California coast with major stops at San Francisco, Los Angeles, and San Diego. Each place is represented by pictures, postcards and maybe a purchased trinket. Take time to sit together on the floor and lay out the display and play the "I remember when . . ." game. This is also good practice in sorting by time sequence and geographical location (Figure 14.1).

You may not want a pile of souvenirs on the living room floor as a permanent arrangement. Fitting new collections into the old décor can be an adjustment. Nevertheless, clearing a shelf in a child's room makes it possible to group all the souvenirs in one place for review. It may not "fit the décor" and it may be messy for a while, but it encourages unified thinking. Certainly it helps when a child is faced with the inevitable, "Tell Aunt Nancy what you saw on your trip."

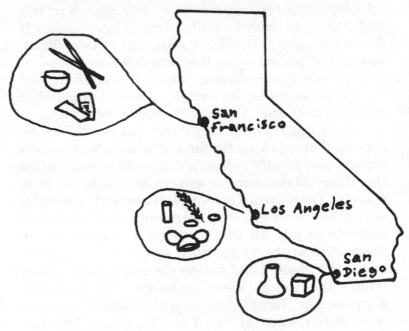

Figure 14.1. Lay out a display

Group some of the pretty natural items together for a special effect. Pour some wet but stiff Plaster-of-Paris on some wax paper. Arrange some items attractively—perhaps a beach arrangement of two or three stones, smoothed by the surf, and a shell lying in front of an upright gull's feather or two, surrounded by a short length of weathered boat rope.

Writing down a memory helps a child organize his thoughts. Children's stories and memories, illustrated with pictures, make lovely mementos. When a child visits an historical place, ask him to imagine and write about what it might have been like "way back when."

After a brief visit to an abandoned one-room schoolhouse (Figure 14.2), Mary and David thought about what it would have been like to go to school there over seventy years ago. Mary wasn't

Figure 14.2. Abandoned one-room schoolhouse

old enough to write a story, but she drew a picture (Figure 14.3) and explained, "It's lonely there now, but once there were lots of children. The teacher is inside." Not great art nor a fantastic plot, but she realizes that some things were different in another time period.

The same concept appears in the brief story written by eleven-year-old David. However, his imaginative powers are more developed than Mary's:

> A while ago I saw a very old schoolhouse. Then I thought about what it would be like to go to school in that time.
>
> One cool spring day I would walk to school. I would look at the trees and the grass as I walked out of my big farmhouse and then look way down the road to the little schoolhouse. Then I would meet my friends and walk to school. While at school I would hang my coat on a hook in the hall and go sit down near a black stove and some blackboards.
>
> The school is quiet now. A bird built a nest over the door.

Different types of experience require different writing styles. The children visited the Open House Tour of Lock and Dam Number 9 on the Mississippi River. On this trip they observed a process in action. Barges moved into the lock and water was pumped in until the barges were able to move north across a higher level of water. The children also saw the large roller gates on the dam which can be raised and lowered with huge machine-driven chains, resembling bicycle chains (Fig. 14.4). Mary reported her experience orally:

> I saw a lock open. Then a dam open. I got to go over one of those lock bridges. Then I got to go in a building and see the dam open up. I got to see the chain that looks like a bike chain. Then we went out of the building. I saw a boat

Figure 14.3. Mary's picture of school in "the old days"

Figure 14.4. (a,b,c,d)  Touring Lock and Dam Number Nine on
the Mississippi River

come through the lock. We got to see inside of an office. We went right through it and came out the other end.

Her story sequence deals with events as they happened to her, rather than those related to the lock operation.

John's recall is similar but his seven-year-old level of observation is more perceptive:

I went to a dam and saw a barge go through the lock. The barge was empty and was going to get more stuff from the Twin Cities. I think they carry soybeans and coal because I saw a lot of spilled stuff on the barge.

We got to go over a lock and see the dam open by a giant chain. But the best part was the barge going through the locks.

John's story shows evidence that his ability to grasp a sequential set of events goes beyond those events limited to his personal experience. He knows that the barges go north for another load. In order to clarify his thinking, John was asked, "What had to happen in order for the barge to get through the lock?" Here is John's list of steps:

1. A tugboat pushes it through the gates of the lock.
2. The first gate closes.
3. Water starts coming in.
4. The barge gets higher and sways from side to side.
5. They open the front gate of the lock.
6. The tugboat pushes the barge out of the lock.

The aerial photo, shown in Figure 14.5, made it easier for John and Mary to trace the route of the barges as they moved through the locks.

David's description gives more detail of the various parts viewed during the visit:

A few days ago I went to see a lock and dam open house. When we were there, we saw a big barge come through the lock in two pieces. The first piece had nine sections. The second piece had seven sections.

Figure 14.5. Lock and Dam Number Nine as seen from an airplane

Then we went across a bridge to the dam. We went in a tall building and up some stairs. We saw a high crane that ran on a track like a train. Then I saw a big machine that ran the dam parts. The machine had a big bike chain in it. We saw it run and lift the roller gate of the dam.

There was a very nice man that told us about the lock and dam.

His report focuses on cause-and-effect relationships. He noted the size of the barge in relation to the size of the lock, which caused a two-step operation. He also noted the effect of the operating machinery on the dam. He is old enough to follow up his visit by skimming some newspaper reports on the "repair versus replacement" controversy concerning the Mississippi locks. Any extension of a trip experience into adult issues is very valuable to an older child.

But most of all, remembering is fun. These drawings and writings by the children weren't produced for a classroom; they developed out of attempts to clearly remember what they had seen. For a parent, the remembering stage is very important in analyzing your child's level of perception and understanding.

Remembering helps pave the way for the next family trip. "Remember the fun we had in Kentucky? Let's go again!" There's the enthusiasm; capitalize on it; every trip will profit the family's memory bank, and your children's education.

# Bibliography

Aikman, Lonnelle. *We the People*. Washington, D. C.: The United States Capitol Historical Society, 1963.

Bunker, Barbara B., et al. *A Student's Guide to Conducting Social Science Research*. New York: Human Sciences Press, 1975.

Burchard, John, and Albert Bush-Brown. *The Architecture of America*. Boston: Little, Brown, 1961.

Dewey, John. *How We Think*. Boston: Heath, 1910.

Dewey, John. *Experience and Education*. Tiffin, Ohio: Kappa Delta Pi, 1938.

Illich, Ivan. *Deschooling Society*. New York: Harper and Row, 1971.

McDonald, Frederick J. "A Concept of Heuristics." In *Research in Teacher Education: A Symposium*, edited by B. Othanel Smith for the American Educational Research Association, Englewood Cliffs, N. J.: Prentice-Hall, 1971.

Phillips, John L. *The Origins of Intellect: Piaget's Theory*. San Francisco: Freeman, 1975.

Piaget, Jean. *Science of Education and the Psychology of the Child*. Translated by Derek Coltman. New York: Orion Press, 1970.

Protheroe, Donald W., and Thomas P. Weinland. *Social Science Projects You Can Do*. Englewood Cliffs, N. J.: Prentice-Hall, 1973.

Reimer, Everett. *School Is Dead: Alternatives in Education*. New York: Doubleday, 1971.

Rudofsky, Bernard. *Architecture without Architects*. Garden City, N. Y.: Doubleday, 1964.

Smith, James A. *Setting Conditions for Creative Teaching in the Elementary School*. Boston: Allyn and Bacon, 1966.

Warren, Roland L. *Studying Your Community*. New York: Free Press, 1965.

Wendel, R. L. "Developing Climates for Learning." *Journal of Secondary Education* 70 (Nov. 1970):330–34.

# INDEX

145